The Complete Putter

The Complete Patter

Michael Munro
Illustrated by John Byrne

Birlinn

This edition first published in 2001 by
Birlinn Limited
West Newington House
10 Newington Road
Edinburgh
EH9 1QS

www.birlinn.co.uk

Reprinted with revisions 2006

ISBN 978 1 84158 128 6
ISBN 1 84158 128 3

British Library Cataloguing-in-Publication Data
A catalogue record for this book is available
from the British Library

Typeset by Palimpsest Book Production Limited,
Grangemouth, Stirlingshire
Printed by Cox & Wyman Ltd, Reading

Introduction

In *The Patter* (Glasgow District Libraries, 1985) my intention was to record in print an impression of the dialect of Scots spoken currently in and around the city of Glasgow. At that time Glasgow's fortunes and self-image were on the rise, and the staging of the Garden Festival in 1988 and the year as European City of Culture in 1990 were both expressions and reinforcements of that improvement. Perhaps my book tapped into this spirit, in any case it seemed to strike a chord with Glaswegians at home and outwith the city, achieving sales to date of over 150,000 copies. In 2005 it celebrated twenty years of being continuously in print.

The Patter made its way all over the world, to wherever exiled Glaswegians had established themselves, from Sweden to Alaska, from Munich to Malaysia. Copies turned up in such august surroundings as the libraries of the House of Commons, the University of Hawaii, and many other institutions of higher knowledge. I had continued to collect vocabulary and in due course a second book was published: *The Patter – Another Blast* (Canongate, 1988). This was also highly successful, if not on the scale of the original volume.

In 1996, feeling that my look at Glasgow language should be brought up to date, I amalgamated the first two books to produce a compendium, which was duly published as *The Complete Patter*. The idea was to unite the best of both volumes, allow me to make amendments and update items that time had affected, and bring into print for the first time the many words and phrases I had since compiled. Neither time nor language development ever stand still, and this new edition of *The Complete Patter* is the fruit of a further ten years of observation, collection, updating and revision. I hope that it will appeal to readers of the preceding books as well as those who come across my work for the first time.

In the intervening years, Glasgow language has been exposed to an ever-wider audience through both the written and spoken word. Writers such as the Booker Prize-winning James Kelman use it naturally to express themselves or their characters. It forms the dialogue of many films set locally, whether made by native directors or those from other places. On television, perhaps the furthest-reaching medium of all, Glaswegian speech has animated many popular comedy programmes, including *Rab C. Nesbitt, Chewin the Fat,* and *Still Game.* Since 2002, Glasgow has even had its own soap opera, *River City.*

For those unfamiliar with all of this Glasgow language, I hope that this book may act as a guide. I have always supported the idea that there is a valid and creative Glaswegian dialect of Scots, which is not, as some would have it, merely a slovenly corruption of English. It may not be pretty; it certainly doesn't shy away from dealing with the less pleasant things in life. However, it is buoyant and resourceful and continues to resist being completely dominated by the forces of linguistic standardisation. If my work contributes towards making this Glaswegian Scots more respected then I will consider it to have been of some use.

I am not in the business of teaching How To Speak Glaswegian. I merely seek to reflect the language that I hear and see around me. While I view this as a serious task, I know from reader reaction that this would be of limited interest without my attempts to amuse in my treatment of the material. Because of this I make no apology for trying to temper scholarship with humour.

As before, the individual words are defined in alphabetical order in the body of the text. There are separate lists for rhyming slang and phrases and sayings, as well as a (brief) look at Glaswegianisms that for various reasons cannot be described as current. The latter is in response to the large numbers of readers who have written to me suggesting such terms, recollected from their youth in the city. While my bias will always be towards current usage, I think it worthwhile to include a few bygone expressions, especially if they seem to have escaped recording anywhere else.

Acknowledgements

It would be impossible to list here all of the people who have made a contribution to this book or its predecessors. My correspondence has been voluminous, originating from all over the world, even Edinburgh, and my personal contacts stimulating and rewarding.

My thanks go now to my wife, Alice, for never-failing encouragement and toleration; to all at Birlinn for their continued belief in the project; and to the citizens of Glasgow who, whether or not they realised they were doing it, supplied me with material. It's their patter.

I would like to dedicate this book to my father, Daniel M. Munro (1921–2001), without whose use and enjoyment of Glasgow dialect I would never have developed an interest in it.

'Apache Land'

a The word *of* often comes out like this: 'A packet a cheese an onion.'

act it Someone who is **acting it** is pretending to be innocent, trying to make another person believe that he knows nothing about what is going on: 'Don't act it, pal. Ah left a full pint standin oan the bar when Ah went tae the lavvy.'

after When a person has recently done something he may describe himself as being **just after** it: 'Naw, Ah couldny go a sweetie, hen; Ah'm just after ma dinner.' 'That's him got his books an he's just after buyin a new motor.'

   What are you after? is a question that might be addressed to you in a pub. This is not a hostile or nosy enquiry but a request as to what you would like to drink.

ah but An expression introducing an objection or contradiction: 'Time ye were in yer bed.' 'Ah but Mammy said we could stay up for *Father Ted.*'

ahead The phrase **go right ahead** is often used to mean have a stand-up fight with another person: 'Ootside, bawheid. You an me're gaun right ahead.'

air When something previously planned falls through or is made impossible by circumstances it may be described as being **up in the air**: 'If this snaw starts tae lie that'll be the fitba up in the air.' The phrase suggests that something has had whatever held it up removed, leaving it dangling without visible means of support, or that something has been sent flying up into the sky as if by an explosion.

airieplane An aeroplane. This is sometimes abbreviated to **airie**: 'Moan, son. Ah'll take ye doon the airport an ye can watch aw the airies.'

Ally Park A nickname for Alexandra Park, a public park in the city's east end: 'Ally Park's the nearest you've ever been to the country.'

amny *or* **amn't** Local versions of *am not*: 'Ah amny comin wi yous.' 'Ah'm getting a lift wi them, amn't Ah?'

am ur This is a strange Glasgow way of emphatically saying *I am*. It usually turns up when the speaker wants to contradict someone else: 'You're no getting wan.' 'Am ur sot.' The negative version of this is **am urny**: 'You're gaun first.' 'No am urny.' It has been suggested that this has its origins in Gaelic but any lexicographical link has yet to be established.

an at A local variant of *and that*: 'She's away tae the shoap tae get mulk an breid an at.' It is also sometimes used to refer to people as well as things: 'Ah'm gaun tae the gemme wi Chas an Doogie an Jackie an at.'

Annacker's midden A proverbial place of mess or disorder: 'Ah wid ask ye in, Mrs Eh, but they weans've got the hoose lik Annacker's midden.' It is occasionally used to describe a person: 'Ye're no gaun oot lik that! Ye're lik Annacker's midden!'

This comes from Annacker's, the name of a former firm of pork butchers, sausage makers, and ham curers. Founded in

1853, at the pinnacle of its fortunes it could boast a chain of sixteen branches all over the city. The company also owned a sausage factory, the last location of which was Napiershall Street (near St George's Cross). The People's Palace has in its collection the shop sign from the Bridgeton Cross branch.

The theory as to how this company earned a place in the dialect goes as follows. Like any food retailer, at the end of a day Annacker's would always have a certain amount of stock that was substandard, damaged or simply stale. Considered unfit for sale, this would be thrown out as refuse. It is said that the hungry poor were given to raking through Annacker's bins for anything edible and the mess this inevitably left gave rise to the phrase.

While Annacker's went out of business in 1942 the saying that the firm inspired lives on in everyday use as a perfect example of how a language clings on to an expression that is vivid and memorable long after its origin is largely forgotten.

Annie Rooney This name is used to mean a fit of bad temper: 'If she finds out you've broken that clock she'll have an Annie Rooney.'

I don't know if this is an example of stigmatising the Irish as being hot-tempered or if there was ever an actual person of this name. Shirley Temple starred in a 1942 film called *Miss Annie Rooney* about a poor little Irish girl, but as I have not had the pleasure of seeing this I can't say whether or not the role involved a lot of shouting the odds.

anything Used as an extreme, if vague, comparison: 'By the time Ah got home Ah wis tired as anythin.'

Apache land A wry description, incidentally illustrating the Scottish West's love of the American West, of any rough or undesirable area: 'That's real Apache land where he stays. The dugs go roon in packs for self-protection.'

appetite Someone who is eating in a particularly hearty manner may have it said of him that **he's lost his appetite and found a horse's.**

Arab A mild term of abuse: 'What are ye hingin aboot ma close fur, ya Arab?' This has got nothing to do with prejudice against asylum seekers or anyone else, and is not in fact racist at all. It probably comes from the old use of the term 'street Arab' to describe someone who, having no fixed abode, lives a nomadic life on the streets.

arm To **put** someone's **arm up his back** literally means to twist a person's arm behind him as a means of coercion. The phrase is often used figuratively: 'It wis his idea tae go. Naebdy put his arm up his back.'

Much stress is placed locally on not arriving empty-handed when invited to someone's house. The idea is to bring a little something for one's host as a token of appreciation, whether this be a carefully chosen vintage wine, after-dinner mints or a bulging carry-out bag. This concept finds expression in phrases concerning the length of a guest's arms, as affected by carrying a heavy weight: 'Ye know oor Davie's no wan tae turn up at sumdy's door wi both erms the wan length.' 'He'd the cheek tae appear at the party wi wan erm as long as the other.'

Armadillo, the A nickname for the Clyde Auditorium, from its alleged resemblance in shape and design to a creature not normally found basking on the banks of the Clyde.

arse **Kick your own arse** is Glasgow's more emphatic version of *kick yourself*: 'Imagine the big chooky tippin us the winner an no backin it hissel! He'll be kickin his own arse the night.' An inept football player may be dismissed by the phrase **he couldny kick his own arse**.

Your arse! is a robust way of saying 'I don't believe what you're telling me' and **your arse in parsley!** means much the same, if rather more poetically expressed. Other than supplying a cheeky wee rhyme I don't know how parsley would come to be intimate with a posterior.

A rude way of telling someone to get lost or stop annoying you is to say **away an take a run up ma arse**, secure in the belief, I'm sure, that no-one will actually comply with the instruction.

Someone who says that he detects an unpleasant odour may provoke the cheeky retort **yer nose is too near yer arse**.

If, on matters of taste, you find that you cannot agree with someone else, you might be moved to tell them **yer taste is in yer arse**.

How's yer arse for lovebites? is the kind of disrespectful remark with which young men like to greet one another.

Someone who is very nervous or on tenterhooks may have it said of him that his **arse is nippin buttons**.

Arse, believe it or not, can also be a verb. To **arse** something is to consume or use it up quickly and greedily: 'Don't leave that gannet wi the carry-oot. He'll arse the whole lot before we get back.' Another sense is to botch something: 'He had a great chance in front of goal but the wee diddy arsed it.' This is, of course, very similar to **make an arse of** something.

arsed To say you **canny be arsed** means you can't be bothered, can't raise the necessary energy or enthusiasm: 'He wants tae go tae the pictures the night but Ah canny be arsed.'

arsepiece To call someone an **arsepiece** is to demonstrate extreme contempt for them.

ask for A shorthand way of sending your best wishes to someone is to instruct a mutual friend to say that you were **asking for** the person: 'If ye see Isa tell her Ah wis asking fur her.' 'Ah ran inty Wee Boaby this morning; he wis askin fur ye.'

at This shortened form of *that* is found in various uses: 'At's terrible at, so it is.' 'Is at so?'

If, when strolling along minding your own business, you hear a cry of **at baw!** this means that a player in a game of football has seen the ball straying in your direction and would like you to retrieve it for him.

at it Someone who is **at it** is doing something illegal or at least underhand: 'Keep yer eye on the guy on the till. Ah'm sure he's at it.'

aw A local version of *all*: 'Ma boots are aw mud.' 'Aw they guys are mental.' 'Aye, an you can sling yer hook an aw.'

away A versatile term. Used on its own as an exclamation it indicates that the speaker doesn't believe what he has just been told: 'Ah see Aileen won the lottery.' 'Away! She never did, did she?' A longer version of this is **away ye go**.

Away is also used in commenting on situations where something occurs that has been expected or is seen as likely to lead to further developments: 'That's her next door comin out to put her thruppence-worth in. We're away now!'

It can also mean leaving or going: 'She's away to her bed.' 'Right, I'll away then.' 'If ye're no for comin Ah'm away masel.'

Someone who appears to be not right in the head, whether through drunkenness or any other reason, may be described as **away wi it**: 'You were away wi it before we even got there last night.' This is sometimes shortened to the first word alone: 'There's nae use talkin tae the bam; he's away.'

Several phrases of rude dismissal begin with **away an . . .** Many are much too offensive to appear here, but some milder examples include:

away an bile yer heid
away an claw yer semmit
away an get yer heid looked
away an gie's peace
away an lie on yer ribs
away an pap peas at yer granny
away an peddle yer arse
away an play in the traffic
away an play wi yersel
away an raffle yer doughnut
away an run.

aye When said in an ironic tone of voice this means that you don't in the least believe what you have just been told. Sometimes **sure** or **right** is added: 'Ah know all the guys in Franz Ferdinand.' 'Aye, right!' 'This is definitely the last time Ah'll ask ye fur a len a money.' 'Aye, sure. That'll be right.' Other more elaborate additions may be used, such as **aye, hooch-aye** or **aye, Popeye**.

A variation is to say **aye, that eye**, which is accompanied by pointing a finger at your own eye. The same meaning can be put across silently (which is handy for sharing disbelief behind the back of a third party) by simply touching your lower eyelid with your forefinger. Perhaps this is related to the old expression 'all my eye', meaning nonsense.

Aye also turns up at the end of queries that exemplify what might be called the Self-Answered Question, e.g. 'Is that your pint, aye?' 'You comin wi us tae Balloch, aye?' The negative of this is seen in such constructions as 'Ye'll no be wantin any dinner, naw?' Is the questioner in such cases 'just checking' and keen to avoid offence, or is he hoping for a contradictory reply? Do you think I know, aye?

Ah'm tellin ye Ah know this joab backside furrit...

B1 *or* **Bee Wan** To **do a Bee Wan** means to go to another place, head off in another direction: 'When Ah seen the big moocher shufflin alang Vicky Road Ah done a Bee Wan up Torrisdale Street.'

This expression derives from a piece of civil service paperwork. At one time it was the procedure that when a person first registered as being unemployed he would be told that no unemployment benefit was available for the first week from the Employment Service. If he was in immediate need of funds he would be issued with claim form B.1 and told to use this to apply for Income Support from the Benefits Agency.

babes To say that something is **the babes** means that it is excellent, just what's required: 'That soup's the babes, Mammy!' An even more affectionate or appreciative version of this is **the wee babies**.

This may well be a product of rhyming slang, with *babes* being shortened from *babes in the wood* i.e. good.

bachle *or* **bauchle** A relatively mild insult aimed at anyone considered old, odd-shaped or slovenly: 'Ah'm no walkin up the road wi a wee bachle lik you!'

back The phrase **at the back of** can mean two things. The more common is in reference to time, where the back of an hour is the period just after it: 'Ah'm meetin them at the back of four.' There's no set length to this period but it would probably not extend beyond twenty minutes: 'You were meant to be here at the back of nine an it's half-nine already.'

The other use is to mean *behind*: 'She left her motor at the back of Woolies.'

All over the back is a phrase used when referring to something considered typical of a person: 'He wouldny gie ye the len a yer bus fare? Aye, that's that stingy aul devil aw ower the back!' It's also used to point out a family resemblance between individuals: 'He's his auld man aw ower the back.'

backie If you help a friend climb over a wall by bending over and allowing him to stand on your back you are giving him a **backie**. The same word is used when a cyclist lets someone climb up behind him on his bicycle: 'Moan Ah'll gie ye a backie up the road.'

backie-in *or* **backsie-in** In an informal game of football in which one side has one more player than the other the outnumbered team may be allowed by agreement to have a **backie-in**, i.e. a player who can double as both goalkeeper and outfield player: 'Okay, yous can have Ronaldinho here an Ah'll go backsie-in fur us.'

backs The area behind a block of tenements is known as the **backs**: 'Ah seen a fox runnin through the backs.' Individually, each close will usually have its own **back court** or **back green**. The two terms are interchangeable but they often reflect whether or not the area is paved or actually has a lawn.

backside furrit Backside forward, or from back to front; like inside out, this means thoroughly or intimately: 'Never mind whit big Bawjaws says, Ah'm tellin ye Ah know this joab backside furrit.'

Bad Boys A disrespectful interpretation of the initials BB, when really standing, of course, for Boys' Brigade.

Bad Fire, the Another name for Hell: 'Ma granny says ma Uncle Joe'll go tae the Bad Fire cause he pit a foreign coin in the collection.'

bad mastard A deliberate spoonerism coined to (narrowly) avoid using foul language: 'Watch where ye're gaun wi that, ya . . . bad mastard, ye.'

badness To do something **for badness** means to do it out of mere spite, to be awkward or for mischief's sake: 'The wee horrur flung hissel aff that waw for badness just cause Ah widny pay attention tae um.'

bad turn To **take a bad turn** means to feel suddenly unwell or faint: 'Is that right, your aul fella took a bad turn comin oot the subway?' This is sometimes shortened to **baddie**: 'Ah took a wee baddie this mornin. Thought Ah wis fur the off.'

bag When someone is sacked from a job this is often called **being given** (or **getting**) **the bag**: 'It's that stupit manager that should be getting the bag, no us.'
   To bag a person is to sack him: 'That's yer last warnin, pal. Any merr a this an ye're bagged.'

-bag This is a common suffix used to label a person who epitomises the undesirable qualities of the word it is attached to, such as *crapbag* (coward) or *grotbag* (unpleasant or dirty person). Other such words include *shagbag, shitebag* and *tossbag*.

baggies *or* **baggie minnies** Minnows, regarded as lawful prey by children: 'Any jamjars, Maw? We're gaun fur baggies in Pollok Park.' Some people also use the term for sticklebacks.

baggy Aggie An insulting name for any female wearing ill-fitting, over-large clothes: 'Hey, baggy Aggie, did ye get that dress at Black's of Greenock?'

bag of rats Someone, usually a child, who is annoyingly lively or who can't sit still may be compared to this: 'Can you no sit at peace till Ah get yer anorak on? Ye're lik a bag a rats the day!'

bag up Any drink that is fizzy and thus fills your stomach with gas is said to **bag you up**: 'She likes that Lambrusco but Ah think it just bags ye up.' 'The wean wis that bagged up wi ginger she couldny eat her dinner.'

bahookie The backside: 'They're no makin jeans that'll go ower that big bahookie.'

baldy Someone who has had his hair cut very short may be described as having **a baldy**: 'Tell that daft barber no tae give ye such a baldy the next time.'

If someone says **I haven't a baldy** this doesn't mean that his hair is long but that he doesn't know anything about the subject being discussed: 'I asked the girl at the Information Desk but she just said "I haven't a baldy".' This is a shortened form of **a baldy clue**, meaning the slightest clue. A similar adjectival use of **baldy** is found in such constructions as **not a baldy one**, meaning not a single one: 'Ah went tae get a wee biscuit for ma tea, an wis there any left? Not a baldy one!'

Baldy Bayne A ready-made insulting name to call a bald man: 'Who are you callin glaikit, Baldy Bayne?' Perhaps there was once a bald man called Bayne who was well enough known to become proverbial. At one time, certainly in the 1980s, there was a pub with this name.

baldy crust The poor old bald man gets it again with this nickname. The term is also used to mean a hairless head itself: 'Ah wis near blinded wi the sun glintin aff his aul baldy crust.'

Balgray, the A familiar name for Balgrayhill, a district on the north side, near Springburn: 'Ah'd like tae go up an see ma wee niece in the Balgray but Ah'm no fit fur that hill.'

balloon A name for someone who thinks his opinions are of such value that they everyone must be given the benefit of them, even though the whole world can see that they are foolish: 'Ye're in a bad way if ye pay any mind tae what that big balloon says.'

baltic Extremely cold, as it can be in the Baltic region: 'Ah'm no gaun oot the day, it's pure baltic oot there.' It must be something about the sound of the word that makes it popular, as opposed to, say, arctic, which would be even colder.

bam To **bam someone up** is to deceive them, or kid them on in some way. More specifically, if a wife, husband or partner **bams up** their significant other, this means they are being unfaithful.

Bam is also used as a shortened version of **bampot**, and this turns up in the inevitable nickname for anyone named Thomas: Tam the Bam.

bammy Like the English version *barmy*, this means insane or daft: 'It wis either you or wan a yer bammy pals that broke the video.'

bampot *or* **bamstick** Sometimes shortened to **bam**, this term is applied to anyone considered 'not right in the head'. This can range from being a bit silly to downright dangerous: 'Gauny chuck that shoutin and bawlin, ya bampot?'

bandit A mildly insulting name, probably just a handy, near-sounding substitute for *bastard* for those who prefer not to swear: 'Ye've made me miss ma bus, ya bandit!'

banjo (pronounced ban-*jo*) To strike someone with one very hard blow: 'We were havin a brilliant night till bawheid decided tae banjo that bouncer.'

bar To **put the bar up** is to ban or exclude a person from a place or activity: 'His maw flung him oot the hoose an noo his Auntie Jeannie's put the bar up as well.'

bare week A week's work without any overtime or bonus: 'Ah've tae pit in a Setterday and Sunday tae get near what pulls in fur his bare week.'

baries To be **in one's baries** is to be in your bare feet: 'They tiles are freezin when ye're in yer baries!'

Bar-L, the Sounding like the name of a ranch from some Western, this is actually one of the nicknames for HM Prison Barlinnie: 'He's daein his Communications Module at the Bar-L.'

barra A local version of *barrow* that appears in various phrases. Someone who thinks highly of himself may have it said of him that he **fancies his barra**. When something welcome or opportune happens to a person he may greet it by saying **that's right inty ma barra.**

A child or a small person that one feels friendly towards is often referred to as **wee barra**: 'Ah think Ah'll pit the wee barra in his buggy an go fur a dauner.' 'Did ye see the wee barra getting stuck inty that big diddy?'

The phrase **Ah've had fruit aff your barra before** is used to mean I'm once-bitten-twice-shy, you don't catch me out a second time.

Barras, the The enduringly popular name for the partly open-air, partly covered market area east of Glasgow Cross. It is proverbially a place to find bargains, and 'Ye wouldny get *that* at the Barras' means that the purchase in question wouldn't come cheap.

The nearby Barrowland Ballroom (known as **the Barraland**) has long been a famous venue for dancing and concerts: 'Ah haveny been tae a gig since The Pogues played the Barraland.'

bassa An altered form of *bastard* which allows people to borrow some of that word's force without technically swearing: 'Ya bassa! Right on ma sore toe!' 'Ach, gie's peace, ya shower a daft bassas!'

bastartin A piece of coarse language whose inventiveness lies in making a noun appear like a verb: 'Ach, chuck the bastartin thing in the bin.'

bat A punch or slap. This is most commonly found in the phrase

a bat in the mooth which is nothing to do with eating a flying mammal but refers to a blow on the mouth: 'Tell yer pal tae watch the language or he'll be gettin a bat in the mooth.'

Baurheid A local pronunciation of Barrhead, a community in East Renfrewshire.

baw A ball, of the spherical playing variety rather than the formal dance.

Ma baw! is a cry in football uttered by a player who wants to take responsibility for playing the ball: 'If ye hear that big nutjob shoutin "Ma baw" just dive oot his road.'

The phrase **the baw's up on the slates** is an expression borrowed from street football, meaning that the ball has got stuck up on a roof and the game cannot continue. In everyday speech it is used of any situation in which something has happened to make progress impossible: 'If this place isny open on a Sunday that'll be the baw up on the slates!'

To **get a kick of the baw** is another soccer-derived expression. In this case it can mean to be given an opportunity, have a chance to make a contribution: 'Aye, it'll be a different story when the other mob get a kick of the baw.'

bawbag The scrotum. Also used as an insult: 'Get oot ma road, bawbag.'

bawface A name applied to someone with a round, full face. Also used to mean such a face itself: 'Ye could spot his big bawface comin a mile away.'

Bawjaws is another, even more poetic, version of this: 'Haw, Bawjaws! Whit aboot some service this end a the bar?'

bawhair A pubic hair, regarded as the very narrowest of fine measures: 'See if ye can move it a bit tae the left. We're just a bawhair aff it.'

bawheid A mildly insulting name to address someone by: 'Watch what ye're daein wi that shovel, bawheid!' It doesn't necessarily mean that the person has a *bawface* but does imply that he is stupid, perhaps suggesting that his head is full of air like a football.

baws Balls, that is, testicles. **Yer baws!** is a fairly direct expression, meant to convey that you think someone is talking nonsense. This can be elaborated into a couple of phrases that mean the same thing, such as **yer baws are mince**, **yer baws are mutton** or **yer baws are cheesy**.

bazooka'd A slang term for *drunk*: 'It's only gone nine an that tube's bazooka'd already.'

bead Someone who is drunk maybe said to **have a good bead on him**.

beamer Someone whose embarrassment is made obvious by blushing is said to have a **beamer**: 'She took a pure beamer when she saw hersel in the mirror.' There are those who like to add to a victim's embarrassment by making a show of how hot the red face is. This is done by licking the index finger, holding it up and making a sizzling noise.

beans **Cool the beans** is an exclamation meaning calm down, take it easy, etc: 'Haud on, cool the beans, eh? It's no as bad as aw that.'

bear This word is used to mean a rowdy or aggressive young man (there seems to be no such thing as a female bear in this context): 'He's no a bad guy, just a bit of a bear.'
   Bears tend to enjoy a good drink and a licensed establishment that they tend to patronize may become known as a **bearpit**: 'That place is a total bearpit on a Friday night.'
   The term is often applied to workers on a building site or oil rig: 'He's the kind of manager that enjoys a crack with the bears after work.'

Bear With a capital letter this is a familiar term for a Rangers supporter. It is happily used by themselves, to the extent that the catering services at Ibrox Park offer a delicacy called Bears Pakora. The term comes from the second part of the rhyming slang for Gers: *Teddy Bears*.

beardie Any bearded man will be referred to as **beardie** by the disrespectful. Also, a father tickling a child will sometimes give the child **a beardie** by rubbing his stubbly face against the kid's smooth one.

beasted Someone who sets about his food in an enthusiastic, if indecorous, way is said to **get beasted in**: 'Nothin wrong wi her appetite anyway, the way she got beasted inty that lasagne.'

beauty When a person is highly pleased by something that occurs he may mark this by crying **ya beauty**: 'The gemme's gauny be on live? Ya beauty!'

bed-recess A feature of many traditional tenement homes, consisting of an alcove or recessed area in a living room or kitchen, originally designed to hold a bed. These beds were often boxed in and could be screened by a curtain when occupied: 'That wee bed-recess came in handy for the boy's computer desk.'

bee Someone who is seen as being absent-minded or easily confused may be called **bee-heidit**. Presumably the idea is that such a person's thoughts fly busily all over the place like bees. A similar comparison is made in the phrase **away wi the bees**: 'Where's the hauf-pun a butter Ah telt ye tae get? Ach, ye're away wi the bees, so ye ur!'

beelin Essentially this means 'boiling', as in **beelin hot**, but it is often used to mean very angry: 'She tried tae keep her face straight when he telt her she wis oot the door but ye could see she wis beelin.'

It can also be used to describe a boil or spot that looks as if it might be about to burst: 'Ye better plook that yin, it's beelin.'

beezer Anything regarded as being an excellent example of its category may be called a **beezer**, but the most common local use is in referring to a very cold day: 'That wis a beezer yesterday; did your pipes freeze an aw?'

bell If someone says he is **on the bell** this means he reckons it is his turn to buy a round of drinks: 'Right boys, the Big Man's on the bell: what are yeez fur?' This probably originated with the old-fashioned pub use of push-button bells on a wall or bar-top (especially in a snug) to attract a bartender's attention.

Bella, the A nickname for Bellahouston Park, a large public park in the southwest of Glasgow, home of the Charles Rennie Mackintosh designed House for an Art Lover: 'This is a good yin of me and yer mammy at the Bella yon time the Pope wis oan.'

It is also the nickname of Bellahouston Academy, a South-Side secondary school: 'Me'n him wis at the Bella thegither.'

belly Someone who is considered to speak without thinking or to talk a load of rubbish may have it said of him that **he just opens his mouth an lets his belly rumble.**

belong to To **belong to** a place means to live there or come from there originally. The most famous example of this is the old music-hall song 'I Belong to Glasgow', but it is used to refer to specific areas too: 'Ah know that guy; he belangs tae Shettleston.'

It is also sometimes used to identify the owner of something: 'Who belongs to this umbrella?'

bender mender A slang term for a stiff drink used as a hair-of-the-dog hangover cure: 'Get this doon yer thrapple. Ye look like ye could do wi a bender mender.'

bendy juice A slang term for alcoholic drink, from the effect this can have on parts of the body, especially the legs.

benson A slang term for a toady or crawler: 'You're always sookin up tae the teachers, ya wee benson.' Apparently this originated from the name of the butler in *Soap,* a popular television show in the late 1970s that was a spoof on soap operas.

berries, the A term used to describe anything excellent: 'This hot weather's the berries!'

berrs, the This means the same as *the berries* and may simply be a shortened form of it.

bet A local version of *beat*: 'Aye, we bet yeez that time an aw.' This is an example of the Glasgow pronunciation shift from the Scots *bate*.

better Two local ways of saying that something is better than nothing are;
> **better than a slap in the face wi a wet haddie**
> **better than a skelp in the baws wi a pun a wet tripe.**

bevvy Alcoholic drink is known as **the bevvy** and a single drink or a session of drinking is **a bevvy**: 'Jist cause Ah like a wee bevvy noo an again disny mean Ah'm an alky or nuthin.'

If one is **on the bevvy** one is in the process of drinking ('Fancy a night on the bevvy?') or one has taken up drinking again after a period of abstinence: 'Two days oot the Royal an that's him back on the bevvy.' Excessive drinking is sometimes called the **heavy bevvy**.

If you like **to bevvy** (drink alcohol) you may very well end up **bevvied** (drunk), and if you are seen to do this often you might attract a reputation as a **bevvy-merchant** (not a licensed grocer but a drunkard).

Bhoys, the A nickname, supposedly indicating an Irish version of *boys*, for Celtic F.C., its players or supporters. This term is happily accepted by the club, as shown by calling its antisectarian drive 'Bhoys Against Bigotry.'

biddy *or* **red biddy** A name given to any red wine that has the combination of strength and cheapness that will appeal to a down-and-out. The term is also applied to the brew resulting from mixing this with methylated spirits: 'Start drinkin that stuff an ye'll end up lyin in a skip swallyin the rid biddy.'

big This is used to mean senior or most important. The **big school** is secondary school: 'Is that you gaun tae the big school in August?' The **big team** is a football first eleven: 'The boss says Ah'll soon be ready fur a run in the big team.'

Big lassie is a child's term of address to an older girl or young woman that they don't know by name: 'Hey, big lassie, you goat the right time?'

Big man is a friendly term of address used to someone the speaker regards as being taller than himself: 'Can Ah get a swatch at yer paper, big man?'

A **big note** is a slang term for a £100 note: 'This is gauny cost ye at least a big note.'

Big Aggie's Man A character from local mythology on whom anything you would rather not own up to can be blamed: 'It wisny me, it wis Big Aggie's Man.' The name is also used in such constructions as: 'Of course it's me! Who did ye think it wis . . . Big Aggie's Man?'

The original Big Aggie and her spouse appeared in a popular song of the 1930s.

Big Red Shed, the A nickname for the Scottish Exhibition & Conference Centre (SECC), from its factory-like red-painted exterior: 'Ageing hippies will be flocking to the Big Red Shed when Neil Young and Crazy Horse attempt to lift the roof in July.'

Billy *or* **Billy-boy** A nickname for a Protestant, especially a supporter of Glasgow Rangers F.C., many of whom use it to introduce themselves in case you're not sure who they are: 'Hullo! Hullo! We are the Billy-boys!' This goes back to King William III (originally William of Orange), military hero of Protestantism.

binger Pronounced to rhyme with *singer,* this is a word used by betting enthusiasts for a losing bet: 'He had five lines on this mornin an evry wan a binger.'

bingo bus A slang term for a police van. Apparently this comes from the police use of *bingo* to mean an arrest: 'Ah seen um getting huckled inty the bingo bus.'

binnies A familiar terms for binmen or refuse collectors: 'She always leaves out a few cans of beer for the binnies at Christmas.'

birlin A Scots word meaning *spinning,* often used locally to mean drunk: 'Sumdy'll need to see Gus up the road. The man's birlin.' There are a couple of more elaborate forms of this, such as 'His eyes are birlin' or 'The eyes are birlin in his heid.'

biscuit tin The proverbial place of safe keeping for the funds of Celtic F.C.: 'The biscuit tin will have to be well raided to cover Parkhead's latest plunge into the transfer market.'

bit A local word for one's home or home area: 'Emdy fancy comin back tae ma bit?'

To **take the bit out of** someone is to exhaust him, leave him out of breath: 'These stairs of yours fair take the bit out of me.'

When it comes to the bit means at the vital moment, the moment of crisis: 'That wee waster'll always let ye down when it comes to the bit.'

black-affronted An almost poetic description of the state of being extremely embarrassed or offended: 'Imagine ma ain daughter no lettin me in her hoose! Black-affrontit wasny in it!'

bladder A term used for a football that is a proper leather one, as opposed to one made of plastic: 'It's no joke tryin to heidie a soakin wet muddy bladder.'

blast A taste or portion of something, especially alcoholic drink: 'See's another blast a that malt, big yin.'

blaw The Scots word for *blow*, used locally as a slang term for marijuana: 'Is he bevvied or what?' 'Naw, too much a the blaw.'

It can also mean an instance of partaking of said weed: 'Ah huvny hud a wee blaw fur ages, man.'

bloodsucker A children's name for a big fat earthworm: 'Ah goat a big bloodsucker fae under a plank an stuck it doon his collar.'

blooter One of the many terms that have crossed over from football into general use. **To blooter** the ball in a game is to kick it powerfully but without much control: 'Staunin there wi an open goal an the big dobber blooters it ower the bar!' The verb can also mean to do something in a quick and careless way: 'There's no way that hoose could be aw painted right in wan day. They must've blootered it.' Similarly, if a person very quickly spends a large sum of money he may be said to have 'blootered the whole lot.'

A blooter is a powerful but unskilful kick of the ball: 'Will Scottish defenders never tire of the big blooter up the park?' It also means a quickly done, sloppy job: 'Look at the runs in this paintwork: this's been a blooter of a job.'

Someone who is very drunk may be described as being **blootered**.

blue Rangers F.C. customarily play in blue shirts and various of their nicknames are testimony to this, such as **the Light Blues** or **the boys in (royal) blue**.

blue job A slang term for a five-pound note: 'That wis a blue job Ah gave ye, by the way, no a wancer.'

bluenose Because of the team's colours, this is a nickname for a supporter of Rangers F.C.: 'We worked thegither fur years an Ah never knew he wis such a bluenose.'

Blythswood Square A city centre location that is highly respectable and businesslike during the day and proverbial for being frequented at night by prostitutes: 'An where d'ye think ye're gaun dressed lik that: Blythswood Square?'

boabie This is used as a slang term for the penis, although why a diminutive form of 'Robert' is chosen is not immediately clear.

boady A local version of *body*. **Gie's a boady!** is a cry sometimes heard at football matches when a fan reckons his team's defenders are not exhibiting total commitment in the tackle.

boat The phrase **just off the boat** implies that a person so described is a recent immigrant from Ireland and is therefore stereotyped as naïve an unsophisticated in the ways of the western metropolis. It is often applied to those who have a look of being of Irish descent: 'Is that her aul fella? He looks like he's just off the boat.'

body swerve Another term from football, where it means the act of getting past an opposing player by quickly moving the whole body out of his reach. In general parlance it is sued to mean any kind of avoiding action or any instance of getting out of something: 'Ah'm that knackered Ah think Ah'll gie the night class a body swerve.' It can also be used as a verb: 'Fancy body-swervin the union meetin an nickin oot fur a pint?' This can occur in the shortened form, **swerve**: 'Didny see ye at the aul dear's party. How'd ye manage tae swerve that?'

bogey The phrase **the game's a bogey** means that because a deadlock or stalemate has been reached (or some other reason has made it impossible to continue) the proceedings in question can go no further: 'If that's yer final offer the game's a bogey.'

This comes originally from the phrase's use in children's games when said by a player who decides the game isn't fair or can't be played properly to the end.

Bogey also used to mean a child's cart (*see under* **Some of Yer Auld Patter**).

bogey rag A somewhat indelicate term for a handkerchief.

boggin A term applied to anything considered foul-smelling: 'Get they shoes oot the bedroom: they're pure boggin!'

boilermaker A disparaging name for a doctor who is regarded as being insufficiently gentle in his handling of patients' bodies: 'That's never a doactor, that. He's a boilermaker.'

boke Vomit. **To boke** is to be sick: 'If ye're gauny boke, gauny try an make it tae the lavvy?' It can also mean to make somebody sick: 'That would boke ye, wouldn't it no?' If something disgusts or exasperates you, you might say it **gives you the boke**. If the thing or person in question is particularly nauseating you might add the word **dry** to this, suggestive of dry retching: 'Don't mention that wummin in ma company; it gives me the dry boke just thinkin aboot her.'

Boke also means the physical product of vomiting: 'How come there's a pile of boke at this corner every Sunday mornin?'

Someone who is feeling nauseous may be described as feeling or being **boky**: 'Make sure ye get a windae seat fur Wee Boky.' If you are **boky-fu** you have made yourself feel sick by eating or drinking too much.

bold To put the words **the bold** before a person's name can be a way of saying that you think he is cheeky or pushy, although this is often used ironically to mean exactly the opposite: 'Well, if it isny the bold Arthur! Is it no past your bedtime, son?'

bolt A perfectly ordinary verb meaning to run away. In Glasgow this has been given a recent twist, being used to command someone to go away: 'Hey you! Bolt! Ye're in ma personal space.'

bomb If someone or something is **bombed out** this means they are rejected: 'He tried tae chat up that big blonde and got totally bombed out.' 'How is it every idea I put up to the committee gets bombed out?'

bonnie A bonfire: 'Mister, kin we go through yer skip fur stuff fur wur bonnie?'

books To **get** or **be given your books** is to be dismissed from your job: 'When he turned up on the Monday mornin they just gave him his books.'

boolin, the The game of bowling (on grass, not the ten-pin variety) or an occasion of this: 'He's wantin his good blazer dry-cleaned for the boolin.'

boona If you **give it the full boona** this means that you go the whole hog, hold nothing back, particularly in a situation in which you might as well be hung for a sheep as a lamb: 'Are ye for the off after this pint, or are we gauny gie it the full boona the night?'

The expression entered the dialect from Indian and Pakistani restaurants where if you order a dish called a boona (as in a lamb boona, chicken boona, etc) the sauce is drier and thicker than in a standard curry. In some restaurants it is possible to order a half boona or a full boona, depending on how the size of your eyes relates to that of your belly.

boot To boot someone can mean to sack him: 'She wis workin in that newsagent's but she got bootit fur eatin the rolls.'

To **put** or **stick the boot on** someone is to kick him: 'Ah seen two boays puttin the boot on an aul jakey.'

Boots' Corner Although the corner of Union Street and Argyle Street is no longer occupied by Boots the Chemist, this handy place for dating couples to meet is still referred to by the old name. It is also known as **Dizzy Corner**.

booze cruise A pleasure cruise down the Clyde or on a loch or canal during which it is understood that there will be substantial splicing of the mainbrace. Far from trying to live down such a nickname, some companies offering the service actually use the term in their advertising.

bothy This rural term for a shepherd's hut or farm workers' bunkhouse is used in urban contexts for any temporary shelter for workmen, including the portable constructions that have electricity, running water, telephones and even wireless internet connections. It is even used to mean the workers' cloakroom/toilet area in a factory: 'Ah don't care if it's chuckin it doon: youse're no peyed tae sit playin kerds in this bothy aw day!'

bought house A home that is privately owned rather than rented: 'Ma son an his wife are getting on great – they stay in a bought hoose noo, ye know.'

bowf If something is very smelly it may be described as **bowfin**: 'Ah'll need tae clean oot that fridge. There's somethin bowfin in there.'

A **bowf** is a stink or nasty smell, and a particularly sickening example of this is often called a **honkin bowf**.

bowfies A local term for head lice: 'Miss, can Ah no sit next tae him? His heid's full a bowfies, so it is.' There must be a connection between this and **bowf**.

bowly Pronounced so that the 'bow' rhymes with 'cow', this means bandy-legged: 'Ah'm gaun bowly wi humphin that wean up the stair.'

box Used as a slang term for the head in such phrases as **out ma box** which means very drunk or incapacitated by drugs. If something **does your box in** this means it is beyond your powers of comprehension: 'Miss, they irregular verbs are pure daein ma box in. Could ye no just read us a story?'

brain Someone who is described as being **out his brain** is totally intoxicated: 'Ah canny remember getting hame last night. Must've been right oot ma brain.' **Brainless** is used in a similar way.

A contemptuous way of referring to a no-scoring draw in football is to say **nae brains each**.

brammed-up Dressed in your best clothes, done up to the nines: 'Ah'm away hame tae get brammed-up fur the dancin the night.' This is obviously related to **brammer**.

brammer A term applied to anything considered a first-class example of its kind: 'Ye should see his new motor; what a brammer!'

bran new A versatile term of approval. It can mean healthy, feeling fine: 'How're ye this mornin?' 'Bran new!' Used of a person it can also mean friendly, nice, dependable, etc: 'You don't have tae worry aboot Rick. He's bran new, that guy.' It is also used as a general term of reassurance: 'Can Ah get ye a drink?' 'Naw, ye're bran new, pal. Ah'm getting them.'

brasser To **take a brasser** means to become embarrassed and blush visibly.

brassneck To **brassneck it** is to try to get away with something by a show of sheer confidence and nerve: 'If they ask ye fur yer ticket just brassneck it an say ye're with the band.'

bree A local word for *brother*. 'Is it okay if Ah bring the wee bree?'

breenge Someone who **breenges** rushes recklessly: 'Ye canny just breenge in there. Ye've got tae make an appointment.'

A **breenge** is an example of this: 'Now I don't want a mad breenge for the door when the bell goes.'

Someone who behaves impetuously may be called a **breenger**.

breidsnapper A slang term for a child, emphasising the aspect of a constant need to keep it fed: 'I hear she's merrit wi a couple a breidsnappers noo.' This is sometimes shortened to **snapper**.

brekwist An odd local variant of *breakfast*. How the *f* became a *w* is anybody's guess: 'Ah like a bit a bacon fur ma brekwist oan ma hoalidays.'

brick A slang term for a pound sterling: 'Gauny stake us ten bricks till the morra?'

bricks If someone is described as being **in with the bricks** this doesn't mean he is on good terms with the building blocks but that he has been present in an organization or establishment since the beginning.

brief A slang word for a car, especially used among those who like to drive away in other people's.

brig This is the Scots word for *bridge* and forms part of some of the place and street names in and around Glasgow, such as The Briggait (the road to the bridge) and Brigton (Bridgeton).

broken pay A wage-packet that has been opened and had some of the money extracted and spent. Traditionally, in households where the woman handles the finances, a male wage-earner will be expected to appear after work with the packet intact to be handed over to her. Men of more dauntless mind might head for the pub first and spend some of their pay before going home. A dominant or fearsome woman may have it said of her: 'Ye wouldny want tae go hame tae her wi a broken pay.'

broo *or* **buroo** A slang term for a Job Centre or Jobseeker's Allowance: 'He's away doon the broo for a restart interview.' This comes from a local pronunciation of *bureau* in Employment Bureau, an earlier name for the government department dealing with this. Any form of benefit paid to the unemployed may be called **broo money** and anyone receiving this is said to be **on the broo**.

bubble To **bubble** is to cry, probably from the image of blowing bubbles from one's nose: 'If ye stop yer bubblin Daddy'll maybe get ye a new wan.' A spell of crying may be called **a bubble**: 'When Ah fun that aul photie Ah jist had tae sit doon an have a wee bubble tae masel.'

Bubbly is a term applied to someone who is crying or in a bad mood: 'What's up with your face, bubbly?'

The Bubbly Babies (crybabies) is a cheeky name for the BB (Boys' Brigade).

bucket This can mean a bin: 'The bucket is all that's good for.' **To bucket** something is to throw it out, reject it as not good enough: 'He took wan look at it an said "Ye kin bucket that fur a start".'

A bucket can also mean a large amount of alcohol: 'You must've had a right bucket last night to end up in a state like this.' To **hit the bucket** means to indulge in a spell of heavy drinking. Someone who regularly drinks heavily may have it said of him that he **takes a good bucket**.

Buckfast commando A slang term for someone who becomes aggressive and fearless when drunk, especially, one presumes, after consuming the well-known tonic wine.

Buckfast Triangle a disparaging slang name for the area of Lanarkshire where it is reputed that sales of the well-known tonic wine are highest. The term **Buckfast Valley** is also sometimes applied to the upper Clyde Valley.

Buckie[1] A familiar name for Buchanan Street: 'Ah seen her runnin up Buckie heading for Queen Street Station.'

Buckie[2] A nickname for *Buckfast*, a proprietary brand of relatively inexpensive, strong tonic wine: 'Ah'm no sayin the boozer wis a bit downmarket but Ah've never seen Buckie in an optic before.'

buckie-up Another term, like **backie**, meaning the use of one's back to let someone climb: 'Ah could get up there if wanny yeez wid gie us a buckie-up.'

budgied If someone's trousers are seen to be too short for him, they may be described as being **budgied**: 'Ah'm needin new jeans, Maw. They wans are totally budgied.' The origin of this usage is not certain, but it could be an echo of an older saying in which someone wearing strides of insufficient extent would be said to be wearing them at half-mast because their budgie had died.

bug To **let bug** is to divulge information, let others in on something not generally known: 'The fly aul devil backs a lottery ticket every week an never lets bug tae her.'

bug-ladders Sideburns, the cheeky implication being that the wearer is infested: 'How d'ye no just let yer bug-ladders grow thegither an cry it a beard?'

Bully Wee, the A nickname for Clyde F.C., who formerly played at Shawfield and are now based at Broadwood, near Cumbernauld. The 'bully' part of the name simply means 'good' (as in 'bully for you'). The club is 'wee' in that it is not on the same level of wealth and importance as the Old Firm.

bum A **bum** is a boaster, someone who goes on endlessly about himself, his doings or possessions: 'And you told me you'd done this sort of thing before. You're nothing but a bum.'

To **bum** is to boast, make empty claims: 'He's always bummin aboot how much dosh he makes.' To **bum your chaff** or **load** is to use your line of patter to talk someone round or pull a fast one on him: 'You'd think he wis God's gift, tae hear him bummin his load.'

To **bum up** something is to praise it, claim that it is excellent: 'That picture wis bummed up tae be the greatest thing since *Whisky Galore* an here it wis mince.' 'He can bum hissel up aw he likes. Ah'm still no impressed.'

bumfle A **bumfle** is a crease or wrinkle in a piece of material or a garment: 'You can smooth out the bumfles in that tablecloth instead of sitting there like a dumpling.' Something that has bumfles in it can be described as **bumfly**: 'Get aff us, you. Ye're gauny get ma good dress aw bumfly.' Some things are more bumfly than others, of course: 'That curtain's no hingin right. It should be bumflier.'

bump[1] Another word for the sack, dismissal from your employment: 'Ah see Wee Doogie goat the bump fae his work the other day.'

bump[2] A slang word with a range of meanings connected with taking something dishonestly, such as swindling, fiddling or defrauding: 'He used tae be a Pools collector till he got caught bumpin the money.' It can also simply mean to steal: 'Miss! Ah canny write cause sumdy's bumped ma pen.'

It is sometimes also used to mean to dupe or fool somebody: 'Ye're wastin yer time if ye think ye can bump me that easy!'

bun For some reason this is used as an insult for a woman, implying she is unattractive or of dubious reputation: 'Seen the wee man's latest burd? A pure bun!'

bunnit This is mainly used for the old-fashioned flat cloth man's cap, but is occasionally used for other types of headgear. In his routine about the Crucifixion Billy Connolly coined the term 'jaggy bunnit' for the crown of thorns placed on Christ's head.

To **do your bunnit** is to become extremely angry: 'He's gauny dae his bunnit if he disny find that ticket.'

The term **bunnit-hustler** was created in the 1970s as a disparaging label for someone who plays up his humble, working-class origins, especially from the comfortable position of being currently well-off or successful.

burny Very hot, whether to the touch or the taste: 'Mind that hot iron, son . . . burny, burny!' 'Can Ah get another wan a yer sweeties, wan a they burny wans?'

buroo A variant form of **broo**.

burst **To burst** someone is to give him a physical beating. It is also found in more specific threats: 'Ah'll burst your arse!'

   To burst a banknote is to use some of its value to pay for something: 'Ye canny burst a twinty fur a newspaper.' 'Ah feel that reckless Ah could burst a fiver!'

   If a betting line, pools coupon or lottery ticket is **burst** this means that it has turned out to be a loser: 'That's me finished wi St Mirren. Two weeks in a row they've went an burst ma coupon.'

   Someone who is in dire need of a visit to the toilet may be described as **burstin**: 'Let us in quick! Ah'm burstin!' This may be elaborated by identifying the particular form of relief required, as in 'Ah'm burstin fur a slash!'

bus The cry **haud the bus!** means wait a minute, slow down, don't be hasty: 'Here, haud the bus! Yer shirt tail's hingin oot.'

   Someone who is referring to a sum of money so small as to be insignificant may say **Ah've lost merr runnin fur a bus**.

but¹ An unusual local form of contradiction involves adding this to the end of a statement: 'She wants tae go tae East Kilbride. Ah'm no fur movin but.' In similar constructions this handy little word takes the place of the standard English *though* or *however*: 'The dinners areny up tae much. Dead cheap but.'

   This kind of thing is found in Autralian English too, no doubt imported along with exiles from this part of the world.

but² A local version of *bit* or *bitten*: 'Your dug's just but ma leg.'

buttie *or* **buttie-up** An act of keeping someone company as they walk along: 'Haud on a wee minute an Ah'll gie ye a buttie up the road.'

buzz **To buzz** is to sniff glue or other solvents: 'The boay's oot his brain buzzin hauf the time.'

bye If you **give** something **a bye** this means you refrain from doing it: 'They're aw gaun fur a pizza the night but Ah reckon Ah'll gie it a bye.' 'Ah thought Ah telt yeez tae gie that shoutin an bawlin a bye!' This comes from the football usage where a team may be given a bye, i.e. allowed to go through to the next round of a competition without having to play a qualifying game, because there is an odd number of contesting sides.

bye kick A goal kick in football: 'The keeper let it go for a bye kick.

That's you clamped!

cakey A fairly mild word used to describe someone regarded as daft, not all there: 'Did you len him a tenner? You're cakey, so ye are!' As with *doughheid* there is an obvious connection with baking, the idea perhaps being that a foolish person's head is like risen dough: full of nothing but hot air.

Cally *or* **Carly** Nicknames for Carlsberg Special, a proprietary brand of strong lager: 'That's three Millers, two Callies, an a vodka an Irn Bru.'

cally dosh A slang term for money: 'Naw, Ah'm stayin in the night – a slight problem wi the cally dosh.'

canny This means *can't*: 'Ye canny shove yer granny aff a bus!'

cargo A slang word for an alcoholic carry-out: 'ye should a seen the size a the cargo they turned up wi!' From this usage, an off-licence is often called a **cargo shop**.

carry-out A **carry-out** is an amount of alcoholic drink or food bought in one place to be consumed somewhere else. The standard English form is *takeaway*: 'That lassie just lifted a bottle out your carry-out.' A **carry-out bag** is the type of plastic bag that pubs supply for takeaway booze, usually emblazoned with a brewer's logo: 'Can you not find something better to hold your swimming stuff than that old carry-out bag?'

The fact that the local pronunciation is often *cairry-oot* has led me to wonder if the name of a pub I once came across, The Kerry Inn, was intended as a pun.

Castle Greyskull A nickname for Ibrox Park, home ground of Rangers F.C. This seems to have come from a children's cartoon series called *He-Man*, but how it came to be applied in this case is not clear.

cattie Short for catalogue, particularly as used in mail-order shopping: 'Did ye get that coat oot the cattie?'

caunle A candle: 'Ah'm no sayin she's getting auld, but when they lit the caunles oan her birthday cake it set off the smoke alarm.' **Whatever lights yer caunle** is a local variant of 'whatever turns you on.'

caur When Glasgow had tramcars they were popularly known as **caurs**. Nowadays the word is used for a motor-car. It is a good example of the local tendency to pronounce the *ar* sound as *aur*: 'It's no faur tae Baurheid if ye've goat a caur.'

caw If you **caw the legs** or **feet** from a person you sweep the legs out from under him. Unsurprisingly, this comes up time and again in football contexts: 'Caw the legs fae that big diddy!'

Celts, the Pronounced *selts*, this is one of the nicknames for Celtic F.C.: 'Oh when the Celts go marchin in . . .'

Central Glasgow Central Railway Station: 'Ah'll get ye at Central at half-seven, under the notice board.'

cerd (pronounced *kerd*) A local variant of *card*: 'Ah pit ma cerd in that puggie a yours an it swallied it!'

chant To sing: 'She's been makin a few bob daein a bit a

33

chantin roon the pubs.' A **chanter** is a singer: 'She's a rare wee chanter, that lassie.'

chanty-wrastler A mild insult composed of two venerable Scots words: **chanty** meaning a chamberpot and **wrastler** meaning a wrestler: 'Tell the aul chanty-wrastler tae get tae his bed an gie us aw peace.' How did this usage arise? The implication could be that the insultee is as despicable as a servant who empties chamberpots, and some people say that seamen in the Merchant Navy often referred to stewards in these terms. It was also suggested to me (by a Professor of English Literature, no less) that the term might describe someone who fastidiously manoeuvres the chanty so as to pee round the rim and thus avoid making a noise. The truth must be out there.

chap **To chap** is to knock, like Wee Willie Winkie: 'Chappin at the windae.' In a game of dominoes, if a player says he is **chappin** he means he is unable to use any of his pieces and has to miss a turn. The player will often signal this by chapping on the table. This gave rise to the phrase, used to dismiss someone as daft: 'Yer heid's fulla dominoes an they're aw chappin.'

In phrases like 'A chap came to the door' or 'There was a chap at the door' the chap is not an unspecified male person but a knock.

character To **give someone his character** is to tell the person exactly what you think of him, never very complimentary: 'She fair gied him his character when he sobered up.'

check When someone wants to draw your attention to something in particular he may do so using a phrase beginning with this word: 'Check the new suit, boys.' 'Check the nick a him!' 'Check that wee burd in the red.'

cheekywatter A nickname for alcoholic drink, highlighting its property of making some people bumptious and at the same time dismissing its effects as none too serious: 'The booze is only cheekywatter tae them. they're inty other stuff for a real buzz.'

cheese it To smile with a big cheesy grin: 'Ah seen you heavy cheesin it when Ah nearly decked it this mornin.'

chib A **chib** is a sharp-edged weapon, such as a knife or a razor. **To chib** soemone is to use such a weapon on him. A **chibbin** is an instance of this: 'Sumdy's gauny get a severe chibbin.' Someone who is known to use a blade in fighting may be called a **chib-merchant**. A **chib-mark** is a scar, as from a wound caused by a blade: 'Check that fur a hard ticket, eh? Chib-marks aw ower the coupon.'

chiefie A friendly term of address for a male stranger, or an affectionate name for a pal: 'Ye finished wi that paper, chiefie?'

chin To **chin** a person is to stop him and speak to him: 'Chin that stewardess for another cup of coffee, will you?'

choke To **choke down** something means to drink it despite having difficulty in swallowing, usually because you have already had enough to drink already or it tastes unpleasant: 'See him an his home-made wine? If ye manage tae choke doon wan gless he thinks ye're wantin anither wan.'

On the other hand, **to choke** a bottle is to drink its contents quickly: 'The perr a them were chokin a bottle a tequila.'

Someone who is very thirsty may describe himself as **chokin**: 'Any danger of some service up this end a the bar? There's guys chokin up here.'

chookie A **chookie** or **chookiebirdie** is a bird, in the kind of vocabulary an adult would use to a child: 'Aw, look at the wee chookiebirdies eatin the breid.'

Chookie is also used to mean a stupid person: 'Think ye can make me look lik a chookie an get away wi it?' The word also appears in phrases that contradict a previous statement: 'He says he'll take it away wi him.' 'Will he chookie!'

chow Pronounced to rhyme with *cow*, this means to chew: 'Ah wouldny say the soup was on the thick side, but ma jaws're sore wi chowin it.'

chuck The phrase **gie it a chuck** means to desist, refrain from doing a particular thing: 'Gauny gie that whingein a chuck?'

chute A playground slide for children: 'That chute's no awfy slidey.'

Citz, the An affectionate nickname for the Citizens' Theatre: 'There's a crackin panto on at the Citz.'

claim To claim a person is to accost him in any of various ways. It can mean to greet someone in a friendly manner: 'I thought I wasn't going to know anybody at the party but Sheila claimed me as soon as I went in the door.' Sometimes the greeting is far from friendly: 'Here's Joey comin. Ah'm gauny claim him for that twinty he owes me.'

It can also be downright hostile, indeed a challenge to a fight: 'Hey bawheid! You're claimed!'

clamp If you tell someone to **clamp it** you are saying be quiet, shut your mouth: 'You've got a big mouth for a wee boy, haven't ye, son? Well, clamp it!'

If you deliver what you consider to be an unanswerable retort to an adversary in an argument you might say to them: 'That's you clamped!'

clapped-in A term used to describe a face that is thin or shrunken-looking: 'That's her faither over there. The wee aul guy wi the clapped-in jaws.' If a person tastes something very sour or hot and the experience causes him to suck in his cheeks a similar expression is used: 'Try a swally a this. That'll clap yer jaws in fur ye.'

clappy-doo Sometimes seen in local fish-shops, this is a kind of large black mussel. The term is often shortened to **clappy**: 'Ye can still get clappies at that wee shoap near The Barras.' The origin of this is Gaelic, from *clab*, meaning an enormous mouth, and *dubh*, meaning black.

Clarence A nickname for someone with crossed eyes: 'What's Clarence's right name anway?' This comes from a crosseyed lion of the same name, star of a popular 1960s television series called *Daktari*.

clatty *or* **clarty** This can mean dirtied with mud, or just plain dirty: 'Don't you dare tramp ma good carpet wi they clatty boots on.' 'Ye should see the state a his hair: pure clatty-lookin.'

A **clat** is a term used for a person considered dirty: 'The wee clat picked a sweetie up aff the grun an et it.'

Clenny, the A familiar name for the City of Glasgow Council Cleansing Department: 'Are you gauny tidy up that bedroom or dae Ah have tae phone the Clenny tae come an clear it?'

A **clenny-motor** is a bin lorry: 'We couldny get up the lane fur that big clenny-motor.'

click To **get a click** means to meet and establish a relationship with a member of the opposite sex. 'C'mon we'll go to the dancin. Ye're not too old yet to get a click.'

Clockwork Orange A nickname, perhaps more popular in the media than in the street, for the Subway. This dates only from 1979, when the system was reopened after modernisation with its trains in a new orange livery.

close In a tenement building the common entrance and hall is known as a **close**: 'The dug's ran up that close.' 'She stays up the next close.' The term is also used to mean all of the individual flats and their occupants considered as a unit: 'She cleans the stairs for the whole close.'

The phrase **up the wrang close** is sometimes used to mean in error, barking up the wrong tree: 'If that's whit ye're after, ye're up the wrang close.'

The **close-mouth** is the street entrance to a close, nowadays often sealed by a door-entry system. The **back-close** is the rear area of a close, leading to the back green: 'Mind we used tae dae wur winchin up a back-close?'

cloy up This means to shut up, stop speaking: 'Gauny cloy up, you?' It is a variant of *clay up*, meaning 'to seal a hole or gap with clay.'

cludgie A familiar term for a toilet, sometimes shortened to **cludge**: 'What's keepin you in that cludgie? Writin yer memoirs?'

clug To **clug** or **put the clug on** someone is to kick them, especially during a football game: 'Sundy needs tae pit the clug on that wee winger.'

A **clugger** is a disparaging term for a defender whose tackles lack skill.

Clyde, the Glasgow's river features in many catchphrases. One of the most popular is used to ask someone if they think you are stupid: **do you think I came up the Clyde on a bike?** The bike can be substututed by other unlikely modes of navigating the river, such as **a banana boat, a coolie boat, a wheelbarrow** or **a water biscuit**.

Someone who is considered unusually fortunate may have it said of him that **he could fall inty the Clyde an come up wi a fish supper** or **wi his pockets full a fish**.

The question **what's that got to do with Clyde navigation?** is a fancy way of questioning the relevance of something someone has said.

Co, the A familiar name for a store owned by the Co-operative Wholesale Society: 'She always gets her messages out the Co.' A peculiarity of Glasgow pronunciation is that the full word 'co-operative' often comes out as 'coa-per-*ait*-ive'.

coal-carry A local name for a piggyback: 'Moan, wee man. Ah'll gie ye a coal-carry if ye stoap greetin.' The expression comes from the days when a coalman would deliver a sack of coal carrying it on his back.

coffin end The narrow end of a tenement building that is tapered (something like a coffin in shape) rather than rectangular: 'The hooses are always wee an poky in a coffin end.'

colour Used as a standard of dirtiness, especially of a person or garment: 'Look at the colour of your shirt. It's manky!' 'Ye should've seen the colour of him when he came in after playin fitba.'

come ahead A phrase used when trying to make someone see sense or change their behaviour: 'Is that aw ye've managed to do? Aw, come ahead, will ye?' It is also a form of a challenge to fight: 'Think ye're hard, eh? Come ahead then.'

come away A cry of encouragement: 'Come away The Spiders!'

coo's arse A term used to describe a mess or a botched job: 'Whoever hung this wallpaper made a right coo's arse of it.' It is used in particular to mean the end of a cigarette that has been over-moistened by the smoker's saliva: 'Okay, ye can have a drag but don't gie it a coo's arse.'

cop To **cop your whack** is to partake of something, whether it be your share, something to eat or drink, or even a good look at something worth seeing: 'Cop yer whack fur a bacon roll before they're aw guzzled.' 'Here she comes noo. Cop yer whack fur *that*!'

The phrase can also mean to die: 'Her aul boy copped his whack at Monte Cassino.'

corrie-fistit Someone described as **corrie-fistit** is left-handed. Such a person may be referred to as a **corrie-fister**.

council telly A derogatory slang term for the basic terrestrial television channels, as opposed to the 57 varieties of mince offered by cable, satellite or digital versions. The idea is obviously that anything that is universally available or bog-standard must be provided by the city council: 'It's a pure shame fur ma granny, she's only got council telly.'

country pancake A kids' term for a cow's dropping: 'What would ye rather do . . . run a mile, jump a stile, or eat a country pancake?'

coup *or* **cowp** To **coup** something is to spill it, knock it over or dump it: 'The big eejit's went an couped the milk jug aw ower the good tablecloth.' 'She sat on the edge of the table an cowped the whole lot.' 'See if Ah catch whoever it is coupin rubbish in that back lane . . .'

To coup out is to fall asleep or otherwise lose consciousness:

'When Ah got up on Sunday Ah fun two guys couped out on the kitchen flerr.'

A **coup** is a rubbish dump: 'Ah'm away tae the coup wi these hedge clippins.' The term is also used for any particularly untidy place: 'That livin room's a pure coup wi all yer toys.'

coupon A slang term for a person's face: 'He had a big daft grin all over his coupon.'

crap **To crap it** means to be scared and lose your nerve: 'When he seen us comin he crapped it an bolted.' A more elaborate form of this is **crap your load**. To **crap it off** someone or something is to be particularly scared of him or it: 'Everybody know you're crappin it aff the gaffer.'

To call someone a **crapper** or a **crap-bag** is to call him a coward: 'Aye, ye better run, ya wee crapper!'

crash When a driver is said to **crash the lights** he deliberately fails to stop at a traffic light that has just turned red: 'Some bampot crashed the lights an went right inty us.'

To **crash ahead** means to carry on with a task without delay: 'You crash ahead wi the undercoatin till Ah get this door-frame sanded.'

crater-face An unkind name to call a person whose face is pockmarked or scarred by acne: 'It's no make-up crater-face needs . . . it's Polyfilla.'

craw To **craw it**, like **crap it**, is to be afraid. Similarly, a **crawbag** is someone who is afraid.

cream cookie A cake, consisting of a sweet bun split and filled with (usually artificial) cream: 'Ah could go a cream cookie wi ma tea, or maybe a wee French fancy.'

cremmy A slang term for crematorium: 'By the look a him it wis a waste a time him comin hame fae the cremmy.'

cuff To defeat, especially in a convincing manner: 'Aye, yer team wis well cuffed the day.'

curer An alcoholic drink taken the morning after a drinking session, intended to dispel the effects of a hangover: 'C'mon for a wee curer an ye'll be bran new.'

Curry Alley A nickname for Gibson Street, in the West End, famous for the number of curry restaurants in what is a fairly short street.

curry-shop A familiar term for any Indian or Pakistani restaurant: 'Phone up the curry-shop an get somethin delivered.'

cutter **To run the cutter** means to act as a bookie's runner or take someone else's line to the betting-shop for him. Apparently this comes from an older use of the phrase referring to smugglers evading the cutter (boat) of the revenue officers.

cut-up A dishonest or 'fixed' outcome to such events as competitions, elections, dividends, or job applications: 'You'd hee-haw chance of getting that job. It was a cut-up from the start.'

Daniel gawpin oot the windae.

Look at dreamy

Must be love, eh?

da Father: 'Is that your da waitin at the bus stop?' 'Want a wee haun wi they messages, Da?'

dabbity A transfer, that is, a design printed on glossy paper that when licked and applied to the back of a child's hand will leave a temporary image on the skin: 'Call that a tattoo? Ah've seen better dabbities.'

The word probably derives from the action of dabbing at the transfer with one's hand to make it print properly.

dale At a swimming pool, **the dale** is the high diving board or platform: 'Gaun! Ye're feart tae dive the dale!'

This probably comes from the local pronunciation of *deal*, the wood used to make such boards, in the same way as *beat* is often pronounced *bate*.

Dale, the A nickname for Leverndale psychiatric hospital: 'Did ye no know he's been in an oot the Dale fur years?'

Dallie, the A familiar name for the Dalmarnock area, in the East End: 'Ah comes aff the plane at Toronto, an ye know who wis the customs man? Wee Charlie fae the Dallie!'

damage To **do yourself a damage** is to injure yourself: 'That wean'll do himself a damage if he dizny get doon aff that waw.'

   Damage is also a jocular term for a person's activities or doings, especially relating to someone enjoying himself in a boisterous manner: 'Naw, Ah no fur gaun hame yet. Ah've a lot merr damage tae dae the night.'

damp *or* **dampt** Words used as substitutes for *damn* or *damned* by those who don't like to be heard to swear: 'Ye've just stood on ma dampt toe, ya stupit-lookin clown, ye!'

Dan A nickname for a Roman Catholic: 'Are ye a Billy or a Dan or an aul tin can?' It is not clear why the name Daniel came to be indentified with Catholic men, as the name is surely common enough among Protestants. Perhaps the well-known Irish song 'Danny Boy' had something to do with it.

dancer[1] A slang term for a landing or floor in a tenement building, e.g. a **three-dancer** is the third floor, a **four-dancer** the fourth floor: 'How is it whenever Ah've tae deliver a new machine it's always a four-dancer?'

   A **tap-dancer** is not, of course, a variety turn in this context but the top (*tap*) floor.

dancer[2] **Ya dancer!** is an exclamation of joy or enthusiastic approval, not addressed to anybody in particular: 'That's us fixed up for the holidays. Ya dancer!'

danger This word is used ironically to mean possibility or chance when it appears that the event referred to is not likely to happen: 'D'ye think there's any danger of your wee brother turnin up on time?' 'Haw, Twinkletoes! Any danger of getting served in here the night?'

   The phrase **no danger** is used to confirm that something is sure to take place: 'Ye'll definitely come an get us?' 'No danger, wee man. Ah'll be there.'

daud *or* **dod** Any piece or portion of something: 'Want a daud a breid wi yer soup?' 'A big dod a concrete fell aff that buildin an nearly kilt an aul wummin.' The bus company Dodds of Troon has unwittingly provided innocent amusement to generations of Glaswegian humorists spotting one of their vehicles and visualising pieces of the seaside resort bowling along the road.

dauner A dauner is a leisurely walk or stroll: 'Fancy a wee dauner doon tae the Toll an back?' **To dauner** is to take such a walk: 'Ah bumped inty yer folks daunerin doon Albert Drive.'

Davie Dunnit A slang nickname for the kind of individual who always claims to have equalled, if not bettered, the achievements of anyone else: 'Ah canny go that guy at aw; he's a right Davie Dunnit.'

dead *or* **deid** In a bar, an unfinished drink that has been abandoned by its drinker is often described as **dead**: 'Is that pint dead?' 'Naw, it's jist no lookin very well.'

dearie mearie A mild exclamation, being a local (and more poetic) variant of *dear me*.

deck The deck means the ground or floor in any context, not just on a boat: 'Who left ma good jaikit lyin on the deck?'

    To deck someone is to knock him down with a blow: 'Rab jumped up an decked the ignorant pig.'

    To deck it means to fall over: 'Ah'll need tae haud on tae you or Ah'm gauny deck it in these heels.'

    To **be decked** is to be laughing so much that you are in danger of falling over: 'We were aw pure decked when we clocked ye wi yer new suit on.'

deefie A cheeky name to call someone who fails to heed what he is told or is, in fact, deaf (*deef*): 'Hey deefie! Did ye no hear me shoutin on ye?'

    To **throw** or **sling** someone **a deefie** is to deliberately ignore him, pretend you were unaware of him speaking: 'Ah said "Hi" tae her in the Post Office but she slung us a deefie, the stuck-up cow.'

deepie *or* **deepo** A schoolkids' term, short for deep trouble: 'You'll be in deepie if the teacher gets ye daein that.'

desperate If someone says he is desperate the most common meaning is that he is in dire need of the toilet: 'Ah'm no sayin Ah'm desperate but ma eyebaws are floatin.'

diddy A **diddy** is a female breast or nipple. The word is also used to mean a fool or stupid person: 'That big diddy hasny got a scooby.' It is sometimes used to describe anything inferior or despicable: 'How come Scotland keeps getting beat by diddy teams?'

    To diddy about or **around** is to behave stupidly or fail to act seriously: 'Chuck diddyin aboot wi they speakers.'

    A **diddywasher** is another word for a stupid or contemptible person, used mainly by schoolchildren. I imagine this comes from being regarded as fit for no more exacting task than washing a baby's dummy after it has fallen on the ground.'

didgy[1] A **didgy** is a dustbin: 'They rollerblades are gaun in the didgy if Ah find them lyin here again.'

didgy[2] Short for digital: 'We've goat didgy telly noo!'

diesel A mixed drink, consisting of lager, cider and black-currant, served by the pint. I suppose if you don't like the taste you can always empty it into your car's fuel tank: 'Ah remember havin three pints a diesel. After that it's emdy's guess.'

dig up To deliberately provoke or goad somebody: 'That toerag's been diggin me up aw night.'

dillion (usually pronounced *dullyin*) A single hard blow, often inflicted using the head: 'Big McConnell gied um a dillion.'

    The word is also used in a wider sense to mean anything exceptionally good: 'Ah'm getting a mountain bike fur ma birthday an it's a pure dillion!'

ding dinner A meal prepared in a microwave oven, which, helpfully, 'dings' when it is ready: 'Ma Maw's workin the night, so that's me fur a ding dinner.'

dinger This word (pronounced to rhyme with *singer*) appears only in the phrase **to go your dinger**. This means to do something very energetically (like *go your duster*) or to lose your temper in a big way: 'Where've ye been to this time? The boss's goin his dinger!'

Presumably it has to do with a bell being rung vigorously.

dingy[1] (rhymes with *thingie*) To **dingy someone** is to ignore them deliberately: 'Ah says "Aw right, Big Man" but he just dingied us.' To **dingy something** is to avoid doing or attending it: 'Not going to college today?' 'Naw, Ah'm gauny dingy it.'

dingy[2] (pronounced *dinjie*) or **dinny** A schoolkids' word for the dinner hall: 'Ah'll get ye at the dinny after this period, right?'

dinner school One might be forgiven for thinking this was an eating academy, but it is actually a school canteen or hall (often known as the **dinner hall**) where lunches are served: 'Would ye rather go to the dinner hall or take pieces?'

dizny This broad Glaswegian version of *doesn't* gave rise to the well-known crack about an inefficient place of work being labelled 'Disneyland' (because such-and-such dizny work, so-and-so dizny work, and so on).

dizzy *or* **dissy** If you make a date with someone and then fail to turn up you are said to have given that person a **dizzy**: 'What's up son, did the lemon curd gie ye a dizzy?'

Some say that this is a shortened form of *disappointment*, but I am drawn to the idea of the stood-up person being left feeling bewildered.

Dizzy Corner A nickname for the traditional meeting place for dating couples at the corner of Union Street and Argyle Street (also known as **Boots' Corner**). So famous a trysting place is this, and so open to the gaze of passers-by, that anyone unlucky enough to have been given a dizzy will be obvious to all and sundry.

doaty *or* **doatery** These words describe a state of forgetfulness associated with old age: 'Just you get yer paws aff yer granda's sweeties, wee yin. Ah'm no so doaty as aw that.'

dobber To call someone a **dobber** is to call them an idiot. It has been suggested that it was originally slang for penis, and if so, it wouldn't be the first word to carry both meanings: 'Ah telt ye Ah wantit decaf, ya dobber!'

dog If you **dog school** you are playing truant (also known as **doggin it**). A **dogger** is a child who is truanting. One way in which schools try to keep track of straying pupils is to issue persistent truants with a **dogger's card**, that is, a card that must be signed by the teacher in charge of each period of the child's timetable. The word is a variant of *dodge* in the sense of *avoid*, and is also seen as part of the term **soapdogger**.

dog's abuse Severe criticism or unpleasant treatment: 'Ye'll need tae get us a delivery a lager right away Ah'm getting dog's abuse aff the punters here.'

dokey To **give it dokey** means to put one's all into an activity, give it laldy: 'We'll need to give it dokey to get this finished the day.'

To **give someone dokey** is to give him a very hard time: 'Her maw gied her dokey fur getting the wean's ears pierced.'

To **take a dokey** is to become extemely angry: 'He took a dokey when he heard he wisny invitit.'

doll An affectionate term of address for a woman or girl: 'How's it gaun, doll, awright?' An **old doll** is an elderly lady, particularly someone's mother: 'She's away up tae see her auld doll.'

done The threatening phrase **you're done** means you've had it, you are doomed: 'See when Ah get a haud a you, pal, you're done.'

doobie A mild term of abuse for someone considered stupid: 'Whit d'ye dae that fur, ya doobie?'

doof **To doof** someone is to punch him: 'He just reached over an doofed him wan.'

A doof is a punch: 'You're askin fur a doof in the coupon an ye're gauny get it.'

doolander A powerful blow: 'What a thump he gave him! A right doolander!'

doolie Another word for an idiot: 'Never mind staunin there like a bunch a doolies.'

doosh A slang word for the face: 'Ah wannered um right in the doosh.'

doowally A slang term meaning an idiot, someone not right in the head: 'There's me staunin oot in the rain lik a doowally an the door's open aw the time.'

This is probably related to the general British slang word *doolally*, meaning crazy, with the influence of the Scots *wally* thrown in.

dot **To dot** is to go somewhere, usually in a brisk manner: 'Ah think Ah'll maybe dot round to Suzy's for a paper.' 'We've been dottin about Shawlands all day.' The term is sometimes used to mean pouring something out: 'Pass us that milk till Ah dot some in ma coffee.'

double dunter 1. An instance of working two shifts back-to-back: 'The gaffer's wantin us tae dae a double dunter the morra.' 2. Any event or undertaking that consists of two parts: 'Saturday night was a double dunter – the pictures then a curry.' 3. Also known as a **double dunt**, a double payment of benefits, perhaps to cover a period of public holiday: 'Wait till ye see. The tube's gauny blaw this double dunter in a week then be after me fur a tap.'

double wide A slang description applied to someone who is extremely fly or not scrupulously honest: 'That boay a theirs is double wide – inty everyhin, knows evrubdy.'

doughball A fool: 'Haw, doughball! That's the wrang queue ye're in.'

dough-heid Yet another term for fool or idiot: 'It wis a hunner-watt bulb Ah telt ye tae get, ya dough-heid!' This some-times shortened to **dough**: 'There it's lyin right beside ye, ya dough!'

dout *or* **dowt** A local term for a cigarette-end: 'Ah hate these people that just open their car door an empty a big pile a douts in the street.'
 When someone has a particularly bad or crooked set of teeth, an unkind observer may say that they have **a mooth lik a rack a douts**.

down Among the betting community **to go down** means to lose: 'Ah backed the favourite in the two-fifteen at Ayr but the donkey went down.' A losing line is described as **down**: 'His pockets were full of lines, every wan a them down.'

draw To call it a draw means to give up a particular activity, call it a day: 'We're getting nowhere here. What d'ye say we call it a draw an head up the road?'

Dreamy Daniel A nickname for a distracted or absent-minded person: 'Look at Dreamy Daniel gawpin oot that windy! Must be love, eh?' Perhaps from the name of a character in a children's comic of the 1960s and 1970s who indulged in fantasies, although it may be older than this.

Drum, the A nickname for the Drumchapel area: 'There's two guys fae the Drum on ma course.' This construction with a shortening of the full name preceded by *the* is a common one used for well-known places or thoroughfares. Other examples include **the Dallie**, **the Mulk** and **the Nitsie**.

Dublin To kick up Dublin means to create a fuss, complain vociferously: 'Ma mammy's kickin up Dublin because he doesny want the wean christened.' Yet another sideswipe at the proverbial hot temper of the Irish.

dummy tit A baby's dummy, or as they are often marketed, soother or comforter. The term was immortalized in the childhood rhyme intended to humiliate a suspected clype:

Tell-tale tit
Yer mammy canny knit
Yer daddy canny go tae bed
Withoot a dummy tit

Some versions of this substitute an even more vindictive second line: *Yer tongue shall be split.*

The phrase **spit out your dummy** means to lose your temper, especially in a childish way, like a toddler in a tantrum: 'Chill oot, man. Nae need tae spit oot yer dummy!'

dump The core of an apple, left after someone has finished eating the fruit: 'Starvin are ye? Want ma dump?'

dumpie A soft or light blow, not seriously intended to hurt: 'Whit's he greetin fur? That wis only a wee dumpie Ah gied um.'

dumps Among children, to **give someone his dumps** is to administer thumps on the back of a person whose birthday it is. One thump per year of age is allowed to each and every child who knows about the occasion.

dundy money A slang term for a redundancy payment: 'Ah say we should fight fur wur joabs. Youse'll no be lang in runnin through yer dundy money.'

dunny A term for the area below a common stair in a tenement building. Such places are proverbial for being dark and spooky: 'Ah dare ye tae go doon the dunny at Hallowe'en.'

duster If you **go your duster** you apply yourself very energetically to a task: 'Finished already? Somebody's been goin his duster!'

They always make me the edgyman cause Ah'm wee and fast...

eachy peachy A slang expression meaning a fair division, equal shares: 'Two tae me an two tae you, that's eachy peachy intit?' This is probably an elaboration of *each*, perhaps influenced by a chant in a children's game which begins 'Eachy peachy peary plum, when does your birthday come?'

easy Usually pronounced *ea-zay*, this is an interjection used to greet any happy event or piece of welcome news: 'Late licence is it? Easy! Here we go boys!' This comes from football, where supporters of a team that is winning effortlessly will often exult in their dominance by chanting 'Easy! Easy! Easy!'

eat-the-breid A nickname, usually more affectionate than disparaging, for a person considered fond of eating: 'C'mon you an me'll have the last two snowballs before big Eat-the-breid comes in.'

ecky A slang word for the drug Ecstasy or a tablet of it: 'There's a guy in the lavvy says he's got good eckies.' **Eckied** means under the influence of this drug: 'Leave her alane, she's eckied oot her brain.'

edgy A term used to mean a lookout: 'Who's gaun edgy?' To **keep edgy** means to keep a lookout: 'The wee man'll keep edgy till you an me have a fag.'

An **edgyman** is someone appointed to keep a lookout: 'They always make me the edgyman cause Ah'm wee an fast.'

I assume the term derives from the nervously watchful condition of the lookout, who must feel 'on edge'.

eejit An idiot: 'The big eejit but a pie straight oot the oven an burnt aw his mooth.' A variation of this is **eejit-heid**.

eekies A term used to indicate a position of equality: 'Gie me a five-spot an that'll be us eekies.' 'Ye can take it or leave it. It's eekies tae me.'

eggs The phrase **all his eggs have two yolks** is said of someone who is always bragging about his achievements or possessions. A variation of this is **all his eggs are double-yolked**.

Eggy Toll A familiar name for Eglinton Toll, a busy road junction and landmark on the South Side: 'Ah says tae the driver "Wan an a hauf tae Eggy Toll" an he looks at us like Ah'm a Martian or somethin.'

eh no? A confirmation-seeking question added to the end of a negative statement. It is roughly equivalent to 'isn't that right?' or 'will you?', as in: 'That's no your motor there, eh no?' 'Don't be late comin back, eh no?'

E.K. Abbreviation and nickname for East Kilbride, offering a saving in time and materials for grafitti-sprayers: 'Rab fae EK.'

El D A nickname for Eldorado, a proprietary brand of fortified wine. The term sometimes also appears as **LD**.

electric soup A familiar term for an alcoholic concoction favoured by those looking for the cheapest, strongest blast, a cocktail of red biddy and meths. The term was adopted as the name for a famous 'adult-humour' comic produced in Glasgow from the 1980s onwards by a crew of merry funsters.

Elky A nickname for any male with the Christian name of Alec. The phrase **get off your elky** means to get up and go, depart: 'It didny take that yin lang tae get aff his elky.'

The full form of the phrase is **get off your Elky Clark**, the last part of which is rhyming slang for *mark*, as in 'get off your mark'. This expression has been around for quite a while, as shown by the details of the man referred to. Alexander (Elky) Clark (1898-1956) was a famous Glasgow boxer, one in a long line of wee tough fighters.

Embra A broad Glaswegian version of Edinburgh: 'Course Ah've been tae Embra – wance.' The Duke of Edinburgh has been referred to for years as the **chooky Embra**.

emdy A truncated local version of *anybody*: 'Kin emdy get a gemme?'

empty When a teenager **has an empty** they have been left alone in charge of the family home while their parents are out for the evening. This is often viewed as an ideal opportunity to invite one's chums round for tea and scones: 'Where are ye gaun wi that cargo, man? Sumdy got an empty the night?'

eppy Short for epileptic fit, as in **take an eppy**. This phrase is also used figuratively, meaning to display bad temper or rage: 'Big Bawjaws'll take an eppy when he sees what wee Tony wrote on the playground.'

erm A local version of *arm*: 'Her erm's aw swole up efter that jag.'

err In broad Glaswegian this is the pronunciation of various words. These are:
air 'All of a sudden an elephant's puddin came flyin through the err.'

Ayr 'He's away tae the racin at Err.' The understanding of this particular pronunciation is vital to appreciating the cheeky remark often addressed to someone warming his backside at a fire, 'Is that yer Ayrshire bacon?' (Is that yer arse ye're bakin?).

there 'Err's wan lyin err.'

evrubdy A broad local version of *everybody*: 'Chuck whingein you. It's the same fur evrubdy.'

ex *or* **exie** Schoolkids' shortening of *excellent*: 'Ah seen that wan. It wis pure ex!'

eyes Bloodshot eyes are sometimes described pictorially as being **sewed wi rid threid**. Another phrase meaning the same, equally graphic if a touch more robust, is **eyes like dug's baws**.

Someone who is so tired that he feels as if his eyes are beginning to cross may say **ma eyes are gaun thegither**.

A face like a Hallowe'en Cake...

face Glaswegians must be great aficionados of facial beauty, judging by the number of ways they have of describing an unattractive face. Here are a few examples:

a face like a bulldog chowin a wasp

a face like a burst couch

a face like a burst tomato

a face like a camel eatin sherbet

a face like a chewed (or **hauf-chewed**) **caramel**

a face like a cobbler's thumb

a face like a Hallowe'en cake

a face like a melted welly

a face like a ruptured hot-water bottle

a face like a wee hard disease

a face like a welder's binch (i.e. bench)

a face like a well-skelped arse

a face like he's been dookin fur chips (i.e. bending too closely over bubbling hot fat)

a face like it went on fire an somebody put the flames out with a shovel

a face like somebody sat on it before it was set/while it was still wet

a face like ye get at Tam Shepherd's (Glasgow's famous joke and trick shop)

a face like ye never sugared his tea

Other ways you might use to say that you find someone less than pleasant to look at include:

ye could chop wid wi that face

ye could roughcast waws wi that face

Someone who suffers from acne or has a good crop of plooks may be said to have **a face like a dartboard.**

A depressed-looking person may be told that he has **a face like a wet Monday** or that his **face is tripping him**. If you have an air of pitifulness or look in need of tender loving care you may be described as having **a face that would get a piece at any windy.**

A **face like fizz** is an angry face, that of someone making no effort to hide their displeasure: 'She just sat there with a face like fizz and never said a word to anybody.'

To **get a sore face** is to be physically assaulted: 'Ye better take yersel aff before ye get a sore face, wee boy.'

Yer face in a tinny! is a phrase used to tell someone that you do not accept what he has just told you. A *tinny* is an old-fashioned tin drinking mug as formerly used by schoolchildren, so perhaps this is an accusation of childishness. The phrase is often shortened to **yer face!**

A crying child may attract the remark **whit a face tae foley a baun**. This implies, I suppose, that only cheery faces should be seen following a band.

Off yer face or **out yer face** are slang terms meaning intoxicated by drink or drugs: 'Whit d'ye mean it wis a quiet night? When Ah met ye ye were pure aff yer face!'

To **moan the face off** someone is to plague him with continual complaints: 'Ah'm getting fed up wi you hingin aboot the place moanin the face aff us.'

faimly Family: 'How's the faimly, okay?'

fair To **go like a fair** means to be very busy, bustling with activity: 'Ah've no had a sit-doon the day. The shoap's gaun lik a ferr.'

Fair, the Although not as universally observed as it once was, the Glasgow fair (the last two weeks in July) is still the annual trades holiday. Most workers will have at least the first Monday (**Fair Monday**) as a holiday and many the preceding Friday (**Fair Friday**) as well. A large number of businesses and factories shut up shop for the whole fortnight and this is a traditional period for getting away from it all: 'That's me booked us up for Turkey at the Fair.'

fairies When a person is described as being **away with the fairies** this means he is distracted, absent-minded, dreaming or just plain silly: 'If ye'd been payin attention instead of bein away wi the fairies ye'd know what to do.'

faither Father. Sometimes used to address an elderly male stranger: 'It's a steep hill this, intit faither?'

falsers An informal word for false teeth: 'No thanks, hen. Ah canny go the toaffees wi these falsers.'

fankle A state of confusion, physical or mental: 'She's got herself into a right fankle tryin to work out what everybody's due.' When something is in such a state it is **fankled**: 'That dampt cat's been playin wi ma knittin an noo it's aw fankled.'

fannybaws A devastating, if a little gender-confused, insult.

far enough The phrase **I could see it far enough** is used when someone can't be bothered with the thing in question: 'Christmas just isny the same wi nae weans in the hoose. Tae be honest wi ye, Ah could see it far enough.' It is sometimes also used in reference to people: 'It's no that Ah don't like them but sometimes Ah could see them far enough.'

fawnty A joke term for a car that is in a poor state of repair: 'He drives a Fawnty . . . fawin tae bits!'

feart This means scared, frightened: 'The wean's feart fae that stupit dug a yours.'

A **feartie** is someone who is cowardly or easily daunted: 'The watter wisny that cauld, but aw they fearties wouldny go in.'

fiddlers' rally The proper meaning of this is, of course, a concert of traditional music played by a massed orchestra of violins. To those who are cynical about the motives and conduct of our local government representatives it is an ironic term for a Council meeting.

filla A fellow; any male person: 'That's a nice big filla she's hingin aboot wi noo.' One's **aul filla** is one's father: 'Me an the aul filla's gaun tae the boolin.'

fine well An unusual construction meaning perfectly or quite well: 'Ye know fine well what Ah'm on aboot, so don't come it.'

Fire Brigutts A slang term for the Fire Brigade, probably an amalgamation of *brigade* and the older word for the Brigade, *butts*: 'Pit that smelly aul pipe oot this minute afore the neeburs send fur the Fire Brigutts.'

fire into To avail yourself enthusiastically of whatever is on offer: 'Fire inty they coffee buns, hen.' 'He said he wis gaun doon the club tae fire inty the lassies.'

Firhill The North-Side home ground of Partick Thistle F.C., the well-known and enthusiastically-supported non-Old Firm Glasgow team: 'Are you joinin the faithful at Firhill on Saturday as usual?' 'Firhill for Thrills' is a catchphrase attached to the stadium, and what curmudgeon would deny that such have been experienced there?

fit Ready to go or do something: 'Is that us fit? Right, off we go.'

five-eight A or **the common five-eight** is a phrase meaning the average person, someone without airs and graces: 'The likes a that's no fur a common five-eight like masel.'

five-spot A five-pound note: 'Gie's that five-spot an Ah'll gie ye two back.' This is American in origin, like a fair number of Glasgow slang expressions.

fix out To organise, whether speaking of physical objects or arrangements: 'It'll take half an hour to get these books fixed out.' 'Give me a bell next week and we'll see if we can fix out another time.'

fizzer A slang word for face: 'What's up wi your fizzer?' This must have some connection with *physiognomy*.

flakie **To take** or **throw a flakie** is to lose your temper spectacularly: 'Yer mammy's gauny throw a flakie if you've not got that room tidied when she comes back.' Some people elaborate on this and talk about a **blue flakie**.

fleein This means drunk, usually in a happy way: 'Listen tae them gigglin! They're fleein, the pair a them!' The term comes from the Scots version of *flying*.

flier To **take a flier** is to stumble over something and fall headlong: 'She didny see the dug lyin in the hall an took a flier ower the bliddy thing.'

flit To move house is **to flit**: 'They wereny in that hoose lang afore they flitted again.' An instance of moving house is called a **flitting** or a **flit**. Someone who is particularly dishevelled may have it said that he **looks like somethin that fell aff a flittin**.

The phrase **a Saturday flit's a short sit**, meaning if you move to a new house on a Saturday you are sure not to be in it long, reflects an old-fashioned superstition. Quite why a Saturday move should be considered unpropitious I do not know.

floaters A collective word for small samples of what you have been eating that find their way into a bottle that you take a mouthful from: 'Okay, ye can get a slug but don't gie us any a yer floaters.'

flute baun A marching band of flute or whistle players, as seen in Orange walks or similar parades: 'Ah never peyed fur aw they music lessons jist so's you could jine a flute baun.'

fly If it is said that someone is **fly for** another person or a thing this means he is up to all the tricks involved in something, well able to avoid being deceived by that person: 'Him? he's no a problem if ye're fly for him.' 'Ye'll pass it the next time, now ye're fly for it.'

Fly can also mean surreptitious, done without letting anyone know about it: 'She nipped out for a fly fag while they were all at the meeting.'

flyman A conman, or at least someone who cannot be trusted: 'Simple Simon met a flyman, goin to the fair.'

fly's cemetery *or* **graveyard** A flat cake, consisting of a thick layer of currants sandwiched between two pieces of pastry: 'Ah canny make up ma mind between the fly's cemetery an a wee Viennese whirl.' The idea is that the currants look like so many dead flies.

folks One's parents: 'When dae yer folks come back their holidays?'

follow-follow brigade, the A collective term for Rangers supporters, from the chorus of one of their best-known songs.

folly *or* **foley** Local variants of *follow*: 'You jump in the aul boy's motor an foley us tae the airport.'

for If someone in a bar asks 'What are you for?' this doesn't mean that they are questioning your role or value in the scheme of things; it is simply a request to find out what you would like to drink. 'Ah'm fur a pie an a pint,' you might well reply.

Similarly, **for** is used to indicate willingness: 'She's no fur havin it.'

Fort Weetabix An irreverent nickname for the St Mungo Museum of Religion, from the Townhead building's wheat-coloured, deliberately rough-hewn stonework.

France A suggested destination for someone you would like to go away, without actually swearing at them: 'Ach, get tae France, you!' 'Away tae France oot ma road.'

frontyways On the model of *sideyways*, this means front-end first: 'Try it sideyways, an if it disny go, take it frontyways.'

frozen snotter A horribly graphic term used to describe some-one who has been out too long in cold, wet weather: 'Come away in oot the cauld instead a staunin there lik a wee frozen snotter.'

full ae it Literally full of it, this means very drunk: 'Man, am Ah gauny get full ae it the night!'

fun A local version of *found*: 'he thought he wis getting away wi it but he wis fun oot in the end.'

Never thought Ah'd see aul Charlie at the garden party. Must be in the grubber right enough...

gallus In Glasgow this is a general term of approval for anything considered excellent: 'Gallus jaikit, wee man!' When applied to people it's more about attitude and includes elements of toughness, cheek, self-assurance and boldness: 'He jist stoats right in through the front door, gallus as anythin.' 'Jist wan a these cheeky wee neds that think they're gallus.'

The origin of the word is *gallows*, and the inference was that a person so described was likely to end up on the gallows or deserved to be hanged. This is an example of a word's meaning ending up as the opposite of what it had originally signified, like the American slang use of *bad* to mean *good*.

game or **gemme** These two forms are interchangeable in most instances, depending on how broad the individual's pronunciation may be. The second version is pronounced with a hard *g*, rhyming with *hem*.

The game or **gemme** is, of course, a game of football: 'We always go to the game on a Saturday.' The phrase **out the game**

comes from this sport, where it describes any player prevented by injury from playing on. In everyday life it is applied to someone who is extremely tired or helplessly drunk: 'Five pints an that wis him oot the gemme.'

People who want to express their approval or encourage someone else in a course of action may say **that's the game**. Conversely, the phrase **that's no the game** indicates disapproval. See also **gemmy**.

gantin If you are **gantin for** something, this means you are particularly keen to have it, whether it is your dinner, a cold drink on a thirsty day, or a sexual encounter.

gantry In a pub the **gantry** is the area (usually shelved) behind the bar where spirits bottles are arranged for display and ease of use, including any bottles mounted in optics. As a collective term it covers the selection of spirits (malt whiskies in particular) offered in the pub in question: 'C'mon next door. The gantry's no so great in here.'

garden party An ironic term for a drinking session on waste ground or in a park, as attended by down-and-outs, alcoholics, or simply those with enough cash for some cheap strong wine or a couple of extra-strength lagers but no place to drink in: 'Never thought Ah'd see aul Charlie at the garden party. Must be in the grubber right enough.'

Gaspipe, the A familiar name for Garscube Road, running between Cowcaddens and Maryhill: 'Whit buses go up the Gaspipe noo, sonny?'

gate To **give someone the gate** is to sack him; similarly, to **get the gate** is to be sacked: 'They wereny long in giein you the gate oota there.'

gaun Go on: 'Gaun doon the chippy an get us a pakora supper.' The word is often used to tell someone to go away: 'Ah'm fed up lookin at ye. Beat it! Gaun!' On the other hand, the phrase **gaun yersel** is intended to encourage someone in what he is doing or to show approval: 'Gaun yersel, Da! You tell the wee bampot!' This probably comes from a football fan's cry of support for a player performing some individual magic.

Gaun can also mean *going*: 'We're aw gaun oan wur summer hoalidays.'

gauny Literally, this means *going to*: 'You're gauny get yer backside skelpt.' When used as part of a request or question it means are you going to, but the idea is really of a firm suggestion rather than a tentative enquiry: 'Gauny see's ower that screwdriver?' 'Gauny shut yer face, you?'

One step further, **gauny no** introduces a request not to do something: 'Gauny no keep bumpin inty us, pal?'

gear The phrase **a bit of gear** refers to a sexually attractive woman: 'Ah widny mind getting a grip a his big sister . . . a fine bit a gear!'

geggie One's mouth: 'Why don't ye just shut yer geggie an no show yer ignorance?' This is sometimes shortened to **gegg**: 'Ah might as well keep ma gegg tight shut as try tae talk sense tae you.'

Formerly, a **penny geggie** was an individual show at a travelling fair. Perhaps the idea of shutting one's geggie is related to closing the curtain on such a stall.

gemme See **game**.

gemmy Pronounced with a hard *g*, this is a term of approval meaning plucky or flash: 'D'ye think it's gemmy tae shout an swerr at yer maw?'

A youth who is seen as gemmy may be called a **gemme kid**.

gen up A phrase used to confirm or question the truth of another statement: 'Ah hear we're getting a rise next month.' 'Gen up?' 'Aye, gen up.'

Gers, the One of the nicknames for Glasgow Rangers F.C. An individual Rangers player may be referred to as a **Ger**.

get Used locally to mean escort or accompany: 'If ye're goin to the shops we'll get ye along the road.' It can also mean *meet*: 'Ah'll get ye ootside the Horseshoe at hauf-six.'

gettin The use of this to mean *becoming* is fairly standard English. What is different about Glasgow usage is that this verb is often transported to the end of the sentence: 'They're kinna snobby gettin.' That is, they're becoming somewhat snobbish.

ginger[1] Any carbonated soft drink may be called **ginger**, often contained in a **ginger boatle**: 'Get us a boatle a ginger . . . Irn Bru or cola.' Perhaps this is a hangover from an earlier time when ginger beer was the only fizzy soft drink available.

Singin ginger is a picturesque term for alcoholic drink, reflecting pithily the predisposition towards song of the well-refreshed: 'Listen tae that racket! They've been at the singin ginger again.'

On meeting a red-haired girl a patter merchant might say **Hello, Ginger, are ye still fizzin?** This is a double play on words, using ginger in the soft-drink sense as well as the nickname.

The phrase **bother your ginger** means to make an effort, show some interest, and is usually found in the negative: 'See that promotion she got? That could've been you, but no, you wouldn't bother your ginger.'

ginger[2] (pronounced with a hard *g*, this rhymes with 'singer') A slang term for a person with red hair: 'Who's that perr a gingers?' 'That's The Proclaimers, ya rocket!'

gingy (pronounced *jin-jy*) A ginger bottle: 'Sumdy wapped us oan the nut wi a gingy.'

gink (pronounced with a hard *g*) A slang word meaning to smell unpleasantly or an unpleasant smell: 'These denims a mine are ginkin.' 'There's some gink in that changin room.'

girth A fat belly, usually of the type produced by devotion to beer: 'Your old boy's got some girth on him since he retired.'

give To **give** someone **into trouble** means to tell them off or land them in trouble: 'The teacher gave me into trouble for gigglin.'

glabber This means mud or dirt and is a variation of the more general Scots *clabber*: 'He slipped in the lane an got his troosers aw glabber.'

glass cheque A jocular piece of slang for a drinks bottle that has a deposit on it and can be used in lieu of cash when returned to a vendor: 'Here son, this glass cheque's yours if ye run oot tae the ice-cream van.'

Glesga *or* **Glesca** Broad Glaswegian versions of the city's name. You will occasionally encounter other variations, such as 'Glasgie' or 'Glasgae', but these are not native to Glasgow, coming instead from other regions of Scotland or from off-target English attempts at a Glasgow accent.

Glesga grin A slang term for a slash on the face: 'Let's see what the Cockney wide boy looks like wi a Glesga grin.'

Glesga nod A slang term for a head-butt: 'Never mind arguin wi the diddy – gie um the Glesga nod.' This is also known as the **Glesga kiss**.

globe Used locally to mean a light bulb: 'That's no another globe went, is it?'

glue The scourge of glue-sniffing has left its mark on the language. If someone thinks you are talking nonsense they might tell you you are **full ae glue**.

go A **go** can mean a fight: 'What's *your* problem, pal? Want yer go?' The phrase **a square go** means a one-to-one fight, unarmed, this being regarded as a fair way to settle a confrontation: 'They think because you come from Glasgow you inevitably end an argument with the offer of a square go.'

  To go can mean to feel like or be in the mood for: 'Could ye go another sandwich, minister?' It is also used in the sense of handle or tolerate: 'Ah canny go the whisky at aw. It gies me the boke.' 'She's nice, but Ah canny go that man a hers.' It can also mean to have the skill or ability to guide and control some kind of vehicle: 'Whit d'ye mean, ye canny go a bike?' Another use is the sense of being able to speak or understand a language: 'Can ye not go the Gaelic at all?'

go-bi-the-waw Literally go-by-the-wall, this is a disparaging name applied to a slow-moving or lackadaisical person: 'We're gauny miss that train if big go-bi-the-waw disny get a jildy oan.'

gommy[1] To call someone a **gommy** is to call him an idiot: 'No that wan, ya gommy, *that* wan.' Someone or something considered stupid-looking can be labelled **gommy** or **gommy-lookin**: 'Ye tryin tae tell us that big gommy-lookin dreep's the gaffer?'

gommy[2] A local version of *gammy*, i.e. artificial, false, as in a **a gommy leg**, or counterfeit, fake, as in **gommy money**.

good This word occurs in various local constructions. The **good room** of a house is one kept for entertaining visitors, containing the best furniture and décor, and not used day to day: 'Ah've telt ye before ye're no tae play in yer Granny's good room.'

Someone who is said to **take a good drink** is a regular heavy drinker: 'She used tae take a good drink but she's aff it noo.'

If an activity is done **good style** this means it is done in an admirable or energetic way: 'We were getting through the carry-oot good style.' 'They're getting on good style wi the decoratin.'

Similarly, to do something **like a good yin** means to do it enthusiastically: 'The wee soul's getting stuck in like a good yin.'

Gorbalonian A native of the Gorbals: 'It was a mixed marriage . . . he was a Govanite and she was a Gorbalonian.'

go through To **go through** a person is to tell him off in no uncertain manner: 'When their faither heard whit they'd been daein he didny hauf go through them.'

Gourock This town on the Firth of Clyde features in the proverbial phrase **away to one side like Gourock**, which means lop-sided, unbalanced, skew-whiff: 'Come here till I fix your hat. It's away to one side like Gourock.' This seemingly derives from the fact that Gourock was built mainly on one side of a hill.

Govan This world-famous district of south-west Glasgow has long since made its mark on the dialect.

Good God in Govan! is an exclamation or mild oath, invented no doubt for the sake of the alliteration rather than the likelihood of the burgh's being chosen as the location for the Second Coming.

Sunny Govan is a nickname for the place, used mainly by the inhabitants, that typifies the Glasgow blend of love of your own patch tempered with ironic realization of its shortcomings.

What's that got to do with the price of spam in Govan? is another of these ways of asking how something is supposed to be relevant.

A or **the Govan kiss** is a slang term for a head-butt: 'He says he walked inty a door but Ah seen um getting the Govan kiss ootside the chippie.'

Govanite A native of Govan: 'Ma Uncle Joe's the secretary of the Sydney Govanites Association.'

gowpin *or* **goupin** This means extremely painful, throbbing with pain: 'Ma erms're gowpin wi humphin awa they messages.' 'That's me aff the bevvy. Ma heid's been goupin aw mornin.'

granda One's **granda** is one's grandfather: 'Say cheerio tae yer granda, girls.' Another form of this is **granpaw**.

granma Grandmother: 'Some a ma granweans cry me Granma an wi some a them Ah get Nana.' **Granmaw** is another version.

granny To say **your granny!** in response to someone else's statement is to imply that he is talking nonsense. It occurs in fuller forms, used to precisely ridicule the other person's claim, as in 'Ma big brother's a brain surgeon.' 'Aye, yer granny's a brain surgeon.' The most popular catchphrases along these lines are 'Aye, an yer granny was a cowboy' and 'Yer granny on a scooter.'

It could be said, though, that in these days when many pensioners live longer and more active lives the idea of Granmaw knocking out the odd prefrontal lobotomy, roping a longhorn, or burning rubber is no longer quite so ludicrous.

grave-nudger A slang term for someone perceived as being a little too long in the tooth: 'You should stick tae the over-30s night alang wi aw the other grave-nudgers.'

greaser A slang word for a lump of spittle and mucus hawked up from the back of the throat and spat out: 'Some clatty article's gobbed a big greaser on this windy.'

Green Lady A familiar term for a Corporation Health Visitor, originally from the colour of their uniform. Although they no longer wear a uniform the term is still in use: 'She's friendly wi Mrs Sloan, ye know, her that's daughter's a Green Lady.'

greet Someone who **greets** is crying. An episode of this may be called a **greet**: 'Just have a right good greet an ye'll feel better.' If someone is feeling less than sympathetic to a person who is crying he may say 'The more ye greet the less ye'll pee.'

Parents often warn fighting children that they are heading for a **greetin match**, meaning that both or all parties in the dispute will end up in tears.

A **greetin face** is one that looks as if its owner has a complaint on his mind or is about to burst out crying: 'Och, what's up wi yer aul greetin face noo?' Anyone who wears such an expression habitually may be called **greetin-faced**: 'Ye canny have a laugh wi that greetin-faced git.'

grey van A vehicle in which, according to folklore, people stigmatised as being insane are transported to secure accommodation: 'If ye carry on lik this it'll be the big grey van that comes for ye.'

The colour of this legendary conveyance sometimes varies from place to place and can be blue or green.

grip If a person is described as having **a good grip of Scotland** this means that they have exceptionally large feet.

The phrase **get one's grip** means to have sexual intercourse: 'He filled her up wi drink so he'd be sure tae get his grip, an here it wis him that flaked oot!'

To **get a grip** of someone is to lay hands on him or her, with a view to embracing, cuddling, and if fortunate even further liberties: 'Check him in the corner. Ah widny mind getting a grip a him.'

If a person needs to be told to calm down or keep the head, he may be advised to **catch a grip, come to grips**, or, with that extra edge of condescension, **get a grip of your liberty bodice.**

grog A local word for *spit*: 'Chuck yer groggin, will ye?' 'There's a big grog on the pavement.'

grot *or* **grotbag** A slang term for an unpleasant or dirty person: 'Get yer paws aff us, ya mockit wee grotbag!'

This comes from the widely used British slang word *grotty*.

grousebeater A slang term for an alcoholic down-and-out: 'There's always grousebeaters hangin about that wee arcade.' This probably comes from cartoon characters used in a series of beer adverts in the 1980s.

growler A **growler** is any person thought to be surly or bad-tempered: 'Oor new maths teacher's a right growler.' It can also mean a dirty look, as in 'What are you givin me growlers for?'

Sausages are sometimes referred to as **growlers**: 'You keep an eye on they growlers while I butter these rolls.'

grun The ground: 'Wait till yer maw sees ye rollin oan the grun in yer good claes.'

gub One's **gub** is one's mouth: 'Ah wisht Ah hudny opened ma gub.' If you want to tell someone to stop speaking you might say **gub it! To gub** a person is to give him a punch in the mouth. The verb can also be used to mean defeat convincingly: 'They'll get gubbed when they come to Parkhead.' An instance of this may be called a **gubbing**: 'We took a gubbin after he was sent off.'

guidie A school term for a guidance teacher: 'Miss, are you gauny be ma guidie next year?'

gums To **bump your gums** is to speak, especially when saying nothing of any importance: 'If youse would stoap bumpin yer gums fur wan minute Ah would tell ye whit we're gauny dae.' The insulting part is of course the suggestion that you are toothless and presumably senile.

gun To **gun** something is to use it up quickly, or, particularly in the case of drink, to swallow it rapidly: 'See that retsina? The only way to drink the stuff is to gun it right back.'

guttered Another word meaning drunk: 'The last time I went out with them I ended up completely guttered.' This probably derives from the idea of a person being so drunk that he falls over and has to lie in a gutter.

gutties A popular name for any variety of rubber-soled soft shoes, especially sandshoes: 'Have ye got gym the day? Mind an take yer gutties.' This comes from *gutta-percha*, a form of rubber used to make such soles.

guy The use of **guy** to mean any male person is much more prevalent in Glasgow than in most other parts of the UK, another illustration of the city's enduring identification with and love of all things American (particularly movies): 'At wee guy stays up ma close.'

. Away an run up ma humph .

hackit An unflattering description, meaning ugly: 'That yin fancies hersel an she's pure hackit an aw.' The term is most commonly applied to people, especially their faces (**hackit-faced**) but is sometimes used to describe things: 'Ah'd rather stay in the hoose than go oot in hackit claes.'

haddie This Scots word for *haddock* is often used to mean a foolish person: 'Ah'm staunin there posin lik a haddie an he canny get his camera tae work.'

hair ile Hair oil, a predecessor of today's hair gel, used as a euphemism for *hell*: 'Whit the hair ile are ye rantin on aboot?'

hairy A **wee hairy** is an abusive term for a young woman considered to be sluttish: 'It's only neds an wee hairies that go to that club.'

A **hairy coo** is a cow of the long-haired Highland breed, familiar to many from toffee wrappers and the paddocks of Pollok Country Park: 'Granda's gauny take ye tae see the hairy coos.'

To **take a hairy fit** (sometimes shortened to **take a hairy**) means to go crazy with anger: 'Your brother'll take a hairy fit when he sees the state you've got his Armani jacket inty.'

half *or* **hauf** A single measure of spirits, most commonly of whisky: 'We've got time for a fly half before we go.' In pubs the actual size of the drink can vary according to whether a bar serves a quarter-gill or something smaller as its standard measure. In less formal surroundings, such as a person's home, the size is totally arbitrary: 'He knows how to pour a good half, your old man.'

Many older pub drinkers will order **a half and a half-pint**, meaning a whisky accompanied by a half-pint of beer.

halfers *or* **haufers** When two individuals agree to buy something between them, sharing the price equally, this is to **go halfers** or **haufers**: 'Ah'll go halfers wi ye on a new DVD player.'

Hallaleen A local variant of *Hallowe'en*: 'When Ah saw the get-up she wis gaun oot in Ah thought it must be Hallaleen.'

hallelujah The **Hallelujahs** is a nickname for the Salvation Army. Someone who joins this organization may be said to **go hallelujah**: 'She an her mother went hallelujah after the father died.'

Hameldaeme Literally, home will do me, this is used as a mythical holiday destination, especially by people who can't afford to go away anywhere: 'If Ah get paid aff it'll need tae be Hameldaeme fur wur summer hoalidays.'

hammer Various phrases are connected with this humble tool. If you want someone else to stop doing something, or turn something off, you might ask them to **give it the hammer**: 'If there's nobody watchin that garbage give it the hammer, for goodness' sake.'

To **put the hammer on** a person is to ask him for a loan of money: 'Ah'm getting scunnered wi him pittin the hammer oan us every Saturday night.'

The hammer's on means that there is trouble on the way

or strict measures are to be enforced: 'The hammer's on just now, so keep your head down for a bit.'

A fine figure of a woman may be described as **well hammered thegither**.

Hampden *or* **Hampden Park** Located on the South Side of Glasgow, this is the national stadium for the Scotland football team and also the home ground of Queen's Park F.C.: 'We're on our way to Hampden, we shall not be moved!' The **Hampden Roar** is the famous noise made by the enthusiastic crowd at international or cup games.

handbaw *or* **haunbaw** This means to lift or carry a heavy load by hand rather than mechanical means: 'Never mind waitin on a forklift. The three ae us'll handbaw this.'

This is probably another import from football, where *handball* is the deliberate illegal use of the hands by any player other than a goalkeeper to play the ball.

handers *or* **hauners** A friend, particularly one who helps out in a fight, is often known as a **hander**: 'Tell yer handers tae keep oot the road an Ah'll gie ye a square go.' To shout 'Handers!' in a fight is to summon friends to pitch in and help. **To hander** someone is to help in this way: 'C'moan an hander us, wan a yeez!'

hang[1] *or* **hing** To **hang** or **hing wan on** a person is to give him a punch: 'On yer way before Ah hing wan oan ye.' To **hang someone's jaw aff his face** is to slash him severely: 'If Ah get a haud a ye Ah'll hang yer jaw aff yer face, ya wee crawbag.'

See also words beginning **hing-**.

hang[2] A common euphemism for *hell*: 'Whit the hang's gaun on here?' 'Ach, tae hang wi the lot a yeez!' 'That's a hang ae a thing, is it no?'

hanks In broad Glaswegian this is a version of *thanks*: 'Hanks a million, pal.' This is one of several examples of pronunciations in which a *th* sound becomes *h*.

happy day A mixed drink, consisting of a wee heavy (small bottle of strong ale) poured into a pint glass, which is then topped up with draught heavy, thus producing a pint with extra kick: 'Gie's a pint a heavy, barman . . . naw, make it a happy day. Ah could do wi wan.'

Happy Larry A proverbially cheery person whose name is ironically applied to any glum individual or killjoy: 'We were aw havin a great laugh till Happy Larry came hame.'

hard-hearted Hannah A jocular name applied to any woman who is relatively strict in her dealings, definitely not a soft touch: 'It's no use askin hard-hearted Hannah for the mornin off just because your budgie died.'

Apparently this comes from an old song about 'Hard-hearted Hannah, the vamp of Savannah.'

hardman A man who is, or wants to seem, tough and violent: 'He's thinks he's a wee hardman but you could kick lumps out of him.'

haud The phrase **haudin up the bar** is a jocular way of describing someone who is leaning on the bar in a pub, as if he was indeed supporting it instead of the other way round: 'Ah might a known the perr a yous wid be in here haudin up the bar.'

hauf-scooped A slang term meaning somewhat intoxicated, rather than completely helpless: 'On yer bike, you. Ye're no turnin up hauf-scooped tae take me oot.'

haun-knittit Literally hand-knittit, this is used to decribe anything that looks ill-made, especially home-made: 'Ah know ma garden sprinkler looks kinna haun-knittit, but at least it works.'

haw A cry used to call for the attention of someone else: 'Haw, Jim! Where's the stop for the fifty-nine bus?'

Hawkheid A familiar name for Hawkhead Hospital, a psychiatric establishment near Paisley: 'Ye'll need tae stoap worryin yersel or it's Hawkheid ye'll end up.'

head *or* **heid** To head is to leave, set off: 'If ye're wantin a lift Ah'm headin in five minutes.'

To put or stick the heid on someone is to head-butt him: 'Mad Boab went an stuck the heid oan the bouncer.'

Keep the head or **heid** is a phrase used in advising someone to calm down. Some people elaborate this into **keep the heid an Ah'll buy ye a bunnit.**

One way of saying that you are suffering with a hangover is **Ah've got a heid lik a sterrheid**, the idea being that your head is pounding as if it was a common landing in a tenement close that endures the tramp of many heavy feet.

There are various phrases containing **head** or **heid** used to tell someone that he is daft or scatterbrained. These include: **yer heid's fulla broken bottles, yer heid's fulla mince, yer heid's fulla magic snowballs** (whatever they are), **yer heid's fulla wee motors.** My personal favourite in this line is **yer heid's fulla dominoes an they're aw chappin** which not only implies that your head is filled with these items but that none of them is any use.

You might also say **yer heid's up the lum** or, if you prefer to be more offensive, **yer heid's up yer own arse.**

One of the dismissive phrases in popular use is **away an bile yer heid.**

A graphic, if unlikely to be carried out, threat is to tell someone he will **get his head in his hands** (**to play with**): 'You'll get your head in your hands to play with if you don't finish that homework for tomorrow.'

If you say of someone (even yourself) **the heid's away** or **the heid's went** this means the person so described has become absent-minded or stupid. It can also mean the person has become vain.

headbanger *or* **heidbanger** A slang term, predating the sense of a headshaking heavy-metal fan, meaning a dangerously unstable person: 'There's no way Ah'm gauny argue the toss wi that heidbanger.'

This is sometimes shortened to **header** or **heider**. The only explanation for the term that occurs to me is that it suggests the person in question is crazy enough to bang his own head against a wall.

heard it! A sarcastic response to any statement or claim that you find hard to believe, the inference being that this is like an old joke that you have been told before: 'That's the first time I've ever been sick through drink.' 'Aye, heard it!'

heart-roastit Someone who claims to be this means that he has become exasperated, worried, or angered by someone or something, especially if the annoyance has been going on for some time: 'Him an his two daft brothers've got their poor mammy heart-roastit wi their fightin an getting inty bother.'

heave, the The **heave** is what you give to a person or thing that you no longer want. This covers such acts as sacking an employee, jilting a lover, ejecting a person from a premises, and throwing out unwanted items: 'Ah see JD's bird gave him the heave.'

heavy bongo'd A slang term meaning very drunk: 'The perr a them wis heavy bongo'd an talkin pish.'

heavy dunt, the Like the heave, this is given to someone or something you want rid of or to something you want to stop: 'If he had any sense he would give that caper the heavy dunt.'

heavy team A collective term for a group of tough individuals, especially a gang. It is often used jocularly to refer to any bunch of people who are supposedly frightening or in authority: 'We better get back to our desks: that's the heavy team coming out of their meeting.'

hector A slang term for a ticket inspector, obviously involving an element of rhyming: 'He got pulled up by the hector on the train tae Balloch.'

heedrum hodrum A disparaging label for traditional Gaelic music and song: 'He says he canny go the heedrum hodrum stuff on the telly, but Ah like tae watch the laddies dancin in their kilts.'

The term comes from the ignorant non-Gaels' attempts to reproduce in words the sounds such music supposedly makes. There's a joke that plays on the term, with a punchline along the lines of: 'You get a haud ae um an Ah'll heider um.'

hee-haw Nothing to do with donkeys, this is a term (meaning *nothing at all*) used by people who prefer not to say *damn-aw* or any even stronger version: 'An whit's in it fur us? Hee-haw!'

heid bummer A rather disrepectful term for a manager or other figure of authority: 'Her aul man's wan a the heid bummers in Weir's.' Funnily enough, there seem to be no different levels of *bummer*: there's no *deputy bummer* or *vice-bummer*, only *heid bummer*.

heidie A **heidie** is a school head teacher: 'That's him staunin ootside the heidie's oaffice.'

It can also mean a header at football: 'The wee man scored wi a divin heidie.'

To heidie something, usually a football, is to strike it with one's head: 'The big twally wasted a perfectly good cross, tryin a bicycle kick when he could've heidied it in nae bother.'

Heidies or **headers** is an informal type of football game in which the emphasis is on heading the ball. **Wee heidies** is a name applied to this when played in a close or other similarly restricted space, or can mean simply one person heading a ball against a wall as a means of improving his heading ability or just to pass the time.

heidnipper Someone who *nips your heid*, i.e. scolds you or harps on about something: 'His aul doll wis such a heidnipper he shot the craw tae London jist tae get away fae her.'

heid-the-baw A nickname that can be applied to practically anyone. While it is often used affectionately, sometimes there is an element of contempt involved; 'Ah thought Big Heid-the-baw would've been here by now.' 'Ye'll get no sense oot a that shower a heid-the-baws!'

Obviously this comes from football, but why someone who heads the ball rather than kicking it should be so patronised I do not know, unless the suggestion is that too many impacts of ball on head tend to dull the brain.

hems To stop a person doing something or to control his behaviour is to **put the hems on** him: 'His folks'll soon put the hems on him when they come back their holidays.' The phrase originally meant putting a collar on a working horse and the meaning has been extended to cover the sense of making something impossible: 'If Ah've tae work late that'll pit the hems oan gaun tae the pictures the night.'

hen A friendly term of address for any female, whether known to the speaker or a stranger: 'Yer wean's flung away his dummy, hen.'

Her, Him Many people refer to their husband or wife not by their given names but by the anonymous pronoun. I use capital letters to show that there is never any doubt as to which particular person is the subject of the discussion: 'Ah just came oot tae get Him somethin fur His dinner.' 'That's me bought the weans their Christmas presents. Ah'll just need tae get somethin fur Her noo.'

here Used as a shortened version of *here is* or *here are*: 'Here Wee Joey on the phone.' 'Here wan here.'

het When children are playing tig, the one whose task is to chase the others is described as being **het**: 'Tracy says Ah'm het but she never touched me.' This is a particular use of the Scots word for *hot*.

hey-you A slang-term for a coarsely-spoken or insolent person: 'Ah'm no too happy wi that crowd she's in wi at school. That wan she brought hame the day wis a right wee hey-you.'

This comes from the tendency of such people to use 'hey you' as the opening remark in a conversation with a stranger.

hielan A Scots word for *Highland*, used to mean illogical, naïve or clumsy: 'Ah'll show ye how tae dae it right, no that hielan way ye're gaun aboot it.' A male native of the Highlands may be referred to as a **Hielanman**: 'Ye canny take the breeks aff a Hielanman.'

Hielanman's Umbrella The stretch of Argyle Street covered by the Central Station railway bridge gained this nickname when it was a well-known meeting place (conveniently sheltered from rain) for Highland emigrants living in Glasgow: 'Ye need tae go alang tae the Hielanman's Umbrella tae get that bus.'

high heid yin A fairly irreverent term for anyone considered powerful or in a position of authority: 'Wasn't he one of the high heid yins in Strathclyde Region at one time?'

hing¹ An equivalent of *hang*: 'She's loast that much weight the claes are hingin aff her.'

The phrase **hing as it grows** (with *grows* pronounced to rhyme with *cows*) is used when something is to be left alone because nothing useful can or should be done: 'Ah've done ma bit. Noo it'll need tae hing as it grows.' The image seems to be of fruit left to develop naturally on a tree.

hing² In broad Glaswegian *thing* is pronounced like this: 'D'ye know the kinna hing Ah'm oan aboot?' When **hing** forms part of another word, like *something, everything, nothing, anything* the final *g* joins the *t* in disappearing altogether: **somehin, evryhin, nuhin, anyhin.**

hing aboot wi A typically unromantic Glasgow expression meaning to go out with, have as one's girlfriend or boyfriend: 'Who ye hingin aboot wi since ye shunted that geek oot the bank?'

hing aff This means get off, let go of me: 'Never mind yer wee cuddle, ya ignorant pig. Just hing aff, wull ye?'

hingie A traditional activity in tenement buildings, to **have a hingie** is to lean out of an open window in a flat and pass the time of day by watching the comings and goings in the street below, occasionally conversing with passers-by or occupants of other open windows. This pastime is becoming less common in this age of the mobile phone and text messaging.

hingin thegither Literally, hanging together, this is a conventional, somewhat downbeat, reply to someone who asks how you are doing. The implication is that things are okay, but no better than that. It can form part of an enquiry to someone who might be considered to be under pressure: 'How're ye the day, young yin . . . hingin thegither?'

hingmy *or* **hingwy** In broad Glaswegian this is a variant of **thingmy**: 'Away an ask hingmy if he'll gie ye a len a that whit-d'ye-cry-it.'

hing oot One way of saying that you are very tired is **ma eyes are hingin oot ma heid**

A **hing-oot** is an insulting slang term for a woman of easy virtue: 'Aye, she's no bad lookin . . . fur a clatty wee hing-oot.'

hingy *or* **hingin** A graphic term applied to someone who, while perhaps not actually ill, isn't feeling or looking very well; 'She's no hersel, the wee soul. She's been hingy aw week.'

hink A local version of *think*: 'Whit d'ye hink a Scotland's chances oan Saturday?'

hit To **have a hit for yourself** is to be conceited, think you're great: 'That boss of yours has got a real hit for himself, hasn't he?'

If someone is likely to forcibly reject something you might offer it may be said that he will **hit you with it**: 'There's nae giein her Gancia if she wants champagne. She'd hit ye with it.'

hoachin This can mean infested with, full of: 'The back garden's hoachin wi wasps.' It can also mean extremely busy, full of people: 'Ye canny get a seat in there on a Saturday night. It's always hoachin.'

hoachy This has the same sense as *jammy*, that is, very lucky, often in a way that is considered undeserved: 'We played them aff the park for nearly ninety minutes then they went an got a hoachy goal.'

holiday giro This is a slang term meaning a double payment of benefit made because of a public holiday, and can be used to mean any unexpected bonus.

Home Ekies Short for Home Economics, as taught in schools: 'Mammy! Daddy wullny eat the sausage roll Ah made um in Home Ekies!'

homer[1] A job done by a tradesman in his own time, as opposed to one carried out as part of his regular employment: 'Ah'll get that done fur ye cheaper than that. Ah know a wee sparkie that does homers.'

homer[2] A football referee who is considered to be favouring the home team in a match: 'No way was that a penalty! The ref's a homer!'

honey A desirable member of the opposite sex: 'C'mon you an me'll go tae the jiggin an get aff wi a perr a big honeys!'
    Conversely, someone considered to be lacking in physical beauty may be described as **no honey**: 'That yin thinks he's God's gift, an he's no honey either.'

honk To honk is to throw up: 'He spent the hale trip honkin ower the side.'
    A honk is an instance of this: 'Ye'll feel better after a good honk.' **Honk** is vomit: 'Aw naw! Ma shoes are aw splashed wi honk!'

honkin A term used to describe anything considered very smelly or simply of poor quality: 'The last party a theirs Ah went tae wis pure honkin.'

hooch Pronounced with the *ch* as in *loch*, this is the exuberant cry uttered by people engaged in Highland dancing or by those looking on: 'With a chorus of hoochs they got stuck into the Gay Gordons.'

hooch aye A term used as the negative of *aye*, intended to imply that something is unlikely: 'Will she pay ye back? Maybe aye, maybe hooch aye!'

hoochter-teuchter An adjective used by Lowlanders to describe Highland or Celtic music, presumably as loved by teuchters who enjoy a good hooch: 'He always wants to go to wan a they pubs that play the hoochter-teuchter music.'

hook To punch, with one hard blow: 'Ah'm no carin how hard he's meant tae be. If he disny shut it Ah'm gauny hook um.'

hooley A term that came to Glasgow from Ireland, meaning a boisterous social occasion such as a noisy house party: 'Man, there's some hooley gaun on up the stair the night.'

Hoops, the A nickname for Celtic F.C., from the green and white hoops on their best-known strip: 'How will he fare in his first season in charge of the Hoops?'

hoor's knickers A disparaging term for Austrian blinds, a silky-looking ruched form of curtains.
    The phrase **up an doon like a hoor's knickers** is used to describe anything that fluctuates: 'The price a petrol's gaun up an doon lik a hoor's knickers the noo.'

hooverin up The practice of going round at a party or other convivial occasion swallowing any unfinished drinks that appear to have been abandoned: 'He wis daein a bit a hooverin up an he took a swally oot a can wi a fag-end in it.'

horse **To horse** something is to do it, especially to eat or drink it, quickly and enthusiastically: 'Dougie an his pals were horsin a few pints before gaun tae the club.' 'If we horse this job we can knock off early.' T**o horse in** or **get horsed in** is a similar way of saying this: 'Horse inty they pies. Kid on ye're at yer auntie's.' **Horse** can also mean to defeat heavily: 'Your team's gauny get totally horsed in the final.'

horse's oranges A picturesque jocular term for horse-droppings: 'If he spies horse's oranges lyin in the road he's out like a shot to snaffle them for his garden.'

hot pea special A portion of marrowfat peas served hot, doused in vinegar, a traditional café delicacy beloved by, among others, the immortal Francie and Josie.

hounded A slang term meaning heavily defeated: 'He's fed up because his team got hounded again.'

how Used locally to mean *why*, which can cause confusion to non-natives: 'How dae Ah have tae go?' With the addition of *no* this becomes *why not*: 'She's no gaun.' 'How no?' Some people elaborate this a little further into **how fur no?**

howlin A slang term meaning very smelly: 'His boots were howlin so Ah slung them oot in the close.'

howpin Another smelly word: 'Jeez-oh! That cheese is pure howpin!'

how's it gaun? Literally, how is it going, this phrase is used as a greeting: 'Hiya Charlie, how's it gaun, ma man?'

huckle To **huckle** a person is to grab hold of him and physically move him from one place to another. This can mean being thrown out: 'Me'n Tam had tae huckle the bampot oot the door before he startit a rammy.' It can also mean being forced inside: 'The polis startit hucklin guys inty their van.'

hudgie To **catch** or **take a hudgie** is to hang onto the back of a moving vehicle, an activity indulged in by reckless children: 'He wis catchin a hudgie oan the back ae a bin lorry an he fell aff an goat hut wi a guy oan a mountain bike.'

Huggy Loch A familiar name for Hogganfield Loch in the East End, often shortened to **Huggy**: 'He tried tae let on he wis an experienced sailor when aw he'd sailt wis an oary boat oan Huggy.'

hughie *or* **huey** To hughie is to vomit: 'That guy looks lik he's gauny hughie in a minute.' **A hughie** is an act of doing this: 'Ah think Ah've goat that disease where ye stuff yer face then have a right good huey.'

The full version of this is **hughie bush**, showing even more plainly that the idea is to represent the sound of vomiting.

hullo! A cry of celebration at some welcome event: 'Hey, Ah think the rain's went aff. Hullo! We're away noo!'

hum-a-ding-dong A slang term meaning very smelly: 'Ah don't know whit's in that bag but it's hum-a-ding-dong!' This is an elaboration of the slang term *hum*, meaning to stink.

humph To humph something is to carry it, usually something heavy or awkward: 'Some hotel this! Ye've tae humph yer ain cases up tae yer room!'

A **humph** is a hump in one's back: 'She'll be getting a humph carryin that wean aboot aw the time.' The word is used in the phrase of rude dismissal **away an run up ma humph.** Another phrase it appears in is **would that no sicken yer humph?** meaning, isn't that disappointing or disgusting. If you are asked to explain your behaviour and find that you have no better excuse for your transgression than it simply occurred to you, you might say **it just came up ma humph.**

A **humphy** or **humphy-backit** person is someone with a hunchback.

Hun A nickname for any Protestant, particularly a Rangers supporter, which is sometimes applied to the Rangers team: 'If the Huns get bate the day the Bhoys'll be top of the table.'

hunner A hundred: 'That jaikit cost us a hunner quid.' The term is often used loosely to mean any large but unspecified number: 'He's been oot wi hunners a different lassies.' 'There's hunners an thoosans a midgies oot there!'

hunt To hurry someone away from a place: 'Ye get nae drinkin-up time in there. They start huntin ye right after the bell.'

It can also mean to get rid of an undesirable person, run him out of town: 'Don't talk tae me aboot cooncillors – they should be huntit, the hale jing-bang o them!'

hurl A ride in or on a vehicle: 'They're away a wee hurl in the new motor.' A stingy person may have it said of him that he is **aye lookin for a free hurl.**

hurtit Someone who gets **hurtit** is injured, whether physically or mentally: 'Was emdy hurtit in that smash?' 'Whit she said pure hurtit ma feelins, so it did.'

hut A local version of *hit* (past tense): 'He hut us first, Miss!'

Hutchie A nickname for Hutcheson's Grammar School: 'I would have expected better from a Hutchie girl.'

huv, hud Local variants of *have* and *had*: 'Youse've no hud tae pit up wi whit Ah've hud tae, neither yeez huv.'

huvtae or **huvtae case** A slang term for a wedding made necessary by a pregnancy, i.e. they *have to* get married.

e grabs a big dod a Irish Steak, slaps it between twa ootsiders an says "That'll need tae dae us till Ah get somethin tae eat."

Ibrox *or* **Ibrox park** The home ground of Rangers F.C.: 'His faither stopped gaun tae the gemme efter the Ibrox Disaster in seventy-wan.'

icey *or* **icie** Short for ice-cream van: 'That tune sounds dead like the one the icey plays.'

Idleonian A rather old-fashioned term for someone who is out of work, particularly if it is suspected that this condition has been chosen rather than imposed. It is also extended to mean anyone who is not pulling his weight: 'Oh aye, here am Ah knockin ma pan in an youse Idleonians can sit an read yer papers.'

ile This Scots version of *oil* turns up in the phrase **away for ile**, applied to anything that is worn out, exhausted or non-functioning: 'Ma aul legs're away fur ile, son!'

indescribables A nickname for pakora: 'Ah'll have a double portion of yer indescribables an gie's plenty sauce, eh Jim?'

inky A school term, used by teachers and pupils alike, for a felt-tip pen: 'Away and ask Mr Mackay for a packet of inkies and come right back here with them . . . and don't run!'

intit no? This literally means 'isn't it not?' and is a common double negative, used by a speaker seeking confirmation of some negative statement: 'It's nae use gaun up north in this weather, intit no?'

into *or* **inty** Various local phrases make use of this term. If you say you are into something this means that you are willing to have it or take part in it: 'Ah'm inty the lamb masala this time.' 'Ah wantit tae go tae T in the Park but she wisny inty it.'

If someone tells you he is **inty your heid** this means that he intends to physically assault you. A person wishing to encourage another to come to blows with a third party may say **inty his heid!** This can be jocular, of course, particularly when a fuller version like **inty his heid wi a teaspoon** is used, making the comparison with smashing in the top of a hard-boiled egg.

Similarly, a football supporter may exhort his heroes to greater commitment in tackling the other side by crying **get inty them!**

Irish steak A jocular nickname, presumably a dig at proverbial Irish poverty, for cheese: 'He grabs a big dod a the Irish steak, slaps it between two outsiders an says "That'll need tae dae us till Ah get somethin tae eat."'

Aw naw, here's a jam sandwich at ma back

jag A **jag** is an instance of being pricked by something, especially an injection: 'Ah hate it when the dentist gies ye a jag in the mooth.' **To jag** is to prick: 'She jagged her finger on the barbed wire.' 'Put yer shoes on. Somethin on the grass might jag yer foot.'

    To jag up is a drug-user's term for injecting oneself with a narcotic.

    Something that is **jaggy** is sharp-pointed (like a jaggy bit of glass) or prickly (like a jaggy nettle).

Jags, the A nickname, punning on the second part of their official title, for Partick Thistle F.C.: 'Of course the guy's a romantic. He's a Jags fan, isn't he?'

jaiket *or* **jaisket** A jacket. To **haud the jaikets** means to be in attendance at some event without taking part, be a witness or onlooker only: 'Don't ask me what's gaun on, pal. Ah'm only haudin the jaikets here.' This comes from the ceremony of a playground fight in which the two combatants have their square go while a supposedly neutral third party takes custody

89

of their jackets and any other restrictive accoutrements.

If someone's **jaiket's on a shoogly nail** this means that his position is not secure, that there is a threat of losing his job. The literal meaning is, of course, that the nail on which the person is accustomed to hang his jacket has become loose, with the result that the next time the person tries to hang up the said jacket it may, along with the nail, fall to the floor: 'Late again, eh? You better screw the nut, sonny boy, cause yer jaiket's on a shoogly nail.'

jake A slang term for methylated spirits (as drunk by alcoholic down-and-outs) or red biddy: 'His guts must be rotten wi aw that jake he pours doon his thrapple.'

A **jake** is also a disparaging term for anyone considered despicable: 'Ah met his pals the other night . . . a right bunch a jakes!'

Jaked or **jaked up** means very drunk, while **jaked out** means unconscious through drunkenness. Both terms have overtones of contempt as they imply that the individuals concerned prefer large quantities of cheap strong drink to a quality tipple: 'It's a wee bit rough an ready, this boozer. Ye'll maybe see wan or two guys jaked oot at a table.'

jakey A slang word for a down-and-out, especially one who obviously drinks lots of **jake**: 'This aul jakey comes up an bites ma ear fur the price of a cup a tea.'

jammy dodger The name of a proprietary brand of biscuit is borrowed in the dialect to mean someone considered to be very lucky: 'Big Dave won a motor in a raffle, the jammy dodger!'

jam sandwich A slang term for a police car, from the Strathclyde force's livery of white with a central red stripe along the length of each side: 'Aw naw, here's a jam sandwich at ma back!'

janny A janitor in a school: 'Here comes the janny wi his bucket a sawdust.'

jarred up Another expression meaning drunk, i.e. having swallowed a few jars (pints): 'It's stupit getting jarred up before the gemme. Ye miss hauf ae it trailin back an forth tae the bog.'

jaur A glass jar: 'Ye'll get a brass screw in that jeely jaur ower there.'

jawbox An old-fashioned term for a kitchen sink. The *jaw* part is a Scots word meaning to pour, and the *box* probably comes from the fact that, especially in tenement flats, sinks were often boxed in to provide cupboard space below them.

jeely Jam or jelly (the preserve rather than the dessert). A **jeely piece** is a jam sandwich and a **jeely jaur** is a jamjar.

Jeely Eater A nickname for an inhabitant of the Vale of Leven, deriving apparently from the time when Irish navvies constructing the Forth and Clyde Canal lived in this area and were said to be so poor that all they could afford to eat were jeely pieces.

jeez-oh A mild oath, obviously a euphemism for *Jesus*: 'Jeez-oh, neebur, whit'll we dae noo?' A similar exclamation is **Jesus Johnnie!** I have no idea who Johnnie might be or how he got dragged into it.

jersey The phrase **sell the jerseys** (sometimes **jumpers**) means to sell out, betray your cause. The origin of this is, of course, football. Any team, but particularly a national side, that plays disappointingly and doesn't seem to want to try very hard, may be accused by disgruntled supporters of having sold the jerseys. In everyday life the phrase may be heard in contexts where people are being represented by others: 'I would just like to remind the chairman that he and the other officials are meant to be goin in tae negotiate, no sell the jerseys.'

jiggin, the Any kind of organised dance, not necessarily involving jigs: 'Ah used tae go tae the jiggin at the Plaza.'

jile A local version of *jail*: 'He should get the jile fur that, so he should.'

jimmies *or* **gymmies** A schoolkids' term for gymshoes or plimsolls: 'Maw, these jimmies're getting too wee fur us.'

Jimmy *or* **Jim** A name used to address any male stranger in a friendly manner: 'What time's the next train, Jimmy?' 'Hey, Jim, is that emdy's seat?'

Jimmy Johnstone When waiting at a pedestrian crossing in Glasgow and the light indicates that you may cross, you might hear someone say: 'C'mom, here's Jimmy Johnstone.' After all, I suppose the much-loved, small-statured former Celtic player was the nearest thing in life to a wee green man.

jiner A local version of *joiner*: 'He calls hissel a jiner but he never served his time.' This comes from the pronunciation of *join* as *jine*: 'Ah hink Ah'll jine the Ermy.'

jink it A slang expression meaning to depart hurriedly: 'Here's the polis, jink it!'

jinkies To say that something is **the (wee) jinkies** is to describe it as excellent: 'Aye, yer granny's trifle's the wee jinkies, intit son?'

jobby The act or product of defecation, also used as a term for an unpleasant individual: 'He's a right wee jobby at times, that yin.' It can also be used as a verb: 'See if Ah get a haud a that cat that jobbies oan ma flower bed . . .'

  The term essentially mean a little job, and when non-Glaswegians use it in the original sense, they unwittingly give no end of amusement: 'I'm just going to do a wee jobby in the greenhouse . . .'

joggies *or* **joggy bottoms** The trousers of a jogging suit, popular as informal wear: 'Ma teacher says Ah've no tae wear ma joggies tae school.'

jooks A slang term for trousers: 'Aw c'moan! Gauny tell that stupit dug a yours no tae jump up oan the good jooks, eh?''

jorrie A glass marble. A game of **jorries** is a game of marbles. This is probably connected with *jaur,* meaning a glass jar. Someone who is seen as speaking poshly or affectedly may be said to **have a jorrie in his mooth**.

jotters To **get** or **be given your jotters** is to be dismissed from your employment: 'If it was up to me the whole lot of ye would be getting yer jotters for this.'

juke If you put something **up your juke** you put it, for concealment or protection, under the front of your outer clothing: 'Here's the teacher comin! Shove that book up yer juke.'

jump If a person associates with a particular person or group he may be said to **jump aboot** with them: 'Is that the guy that jumps aboot wi Mad Boab an aw them?'

Jumpin is a vivid term meaning extremely angry: 'Say nothin tae yer Daddy. He's jumpin awready.'

If a person decides to join in a fight that is already under way he is said to **jump in**: 'Serves ye right. Naebdy asked you tae jump in.'

Jungle, the An affectionate term for the formerly terraced stand at Celtic Park, dominated by the team's most vociferous supporters: 'The massed choirs of the Jungle were already celebrating before the final whistle.' Perhaps because of this, Celtic fans are often known as **Junglies**, although it could equally be argued that this comes from the rhyming slang **Jungle Jim**.

just Like **but** this often appears at the end of a statement, in this case to imply moderation or shortness of time: 'Take wan each just.' 'Ah'll be ready in two shakes just.'

jye A local pronunciation of the letter *J*. It is able to exist side by side with the standard *jay*, which it does not replace in such common combinations as *DJ, OJ, PJs*, etc.

Poor Hughie's gaun aboot like a hauf-shut knife since that wee daft wife's done a bunk.

KB Shorthand for **knockback**: 'Ah hear the boyfriend gave ye the big KB.' This can also be a verb: 'She totally KB'd the big chancer.'

keech Rhyming with *dreich*, this is a term for any kind of filth, but especially excrement: 'Mind yer feet on that dug's keech.' Like other similar words this can be used to refer to a disliked person: 'What's that wee keech sayin noo?'

It can also be used as a verb: 'He says he wisny feart, but Ah bet he wis keechin hissel.'

Keechy is used to describe anything that is filthy, especially if it has been soiled by excrement: 'Sumdy's left a keechy nappy in that bin.'

keekaboo A local name for the game of peekaboo, as played to amuse very young children.

keeker A black eye, from the idea of having to keek out from behind partly-closed eyelids: 'That's a right keeker ye've got.'

keelie Glaswegians are often referred to as **keelies**. Some regard this as an insult, given that the word originally meant a low-class, disreputable person; others adopt the label with pride, but many see it as being morally neutral: 'I really don't know what she's thinking of, bringing a keelie like that to the house.' 'Ah'm a Glesga keelie, born an bred!'

The Highland Light Infantry, a former British Army regiment recruited mainly from Glasgow, was nicknamed the **Glesca Keelies**.

keepie-uppie To play **keepie-uppie** with a ball is to juggle with it, never letting it touch the ground, using any part of the body except the arms and hands: 'Mind Slim Jim playin keepie-uppie wi it at Wembley in sixty-seven?'

kegs A slang term for men's underpants: 'These kegs are stranglin us.'

Kelvinside The archetypal posh area of Glasgow's West End lends its name to the type of refined accent (in which, for example *sex* is what you buy coal in) that often comes across as affected: 'Mai, mai, we're being awfully Kelvinsaide, aren't we?'

kettlebelly A disrespectful name for anyone with a fat stomach: 'Go easy on the pizza or ye'll end up like kettlebelly here.'

keys The cry of **keys!** or **keysies!**, usually accompanied by a double thumbs-up (which is known as having your **keys up**) is used in children's games when a player wants to call a truce or gain temporary immunity from whatever punishment is being dished out. Adults sometimes make ironic use of this when they feel they are being unduly pressurised or berated: 'I was giving him a piece of my mind when he shouted "Keys" and I couldn't help laughing.'

Khyber Pass Another nickname for Gibson Street (see **Curry Alley**): 'We'll dodge down the Khyber Pass an grab a pint in the Doublet.'

kick Someone who **kicks with the left foot** is a Roman Catholic (also known as a **left-footer**). Someone who **kicks with the**

wrong foot is a person regarded in some circumstances as belonging to the wrong Christian denomination: 'There's nae use tryin tae get a joab wi them if ye kick wi the wrang fit.' Oddly enough, there seems to be no equivalent expression about kicking with the right foot. Apparently the saying comes from the idea originating in Northern Ireland that a man digging who uses his left foot to dig the spade in will be a Catholic and the man who uses his right will be a Protestant.

kicking A term used to mean a severe battering: 'They telt him he was on a kickin if he ever went back there.'

kilt A local variation of *killed*: 'A guy up oor close kilt hissel.'

kin A local variant of *can*: 'Kin you no shut up fur a minute?' 'Ye kin whistle fur it.' The negative of this is **kin't**: 'Ye kin jist get yer ain, kin't ye?' Sometimes a double negative appears, using both *kin't* and *no*: 'Ah kin make ma own dinner, kin't Ah no, Mammy?'

kinna A local form of *kind of*: 'Kinna stupit-lookin, in't he?' 'What kinna motor's she got noo?'

kipper's knickers, the A local equivalent of the bee's knees, etc, meaning something wonderful: 'That yin thinks she's the kipper's knickers since Big Joe got aff wi her.'

knacked Like *knackered*, of which this is presumably a contraction, this can mean very tired, broken-down, unserviceable: 'We no near finished yet? We're aw knacked.' 'It's no the tape, it's your video that's knacked.'

knife To describe someone as going about **like a half-shut knife** means that he loooks depressed or introspective: 'Poor Hughie's gaun aboot lik a hauf-shut knife since that daft wee wife a his done a bunk.'

The expression obviously arises from the image of a sad person walking bent over, looking at the ground, compared to a pen-knife with its blade neither fully opened nor properly closed into the handle.

knock **To knock** something is to steal it: 'Who knocked wan a ma pieces?' Someone who steals is a **knocker**: 'Gie's that ruler back, ya wee knocker!'

knock back **To knock** something **back** is to turn it down or reject it: 'The management upped the offer to three per cent but the union still knocked it back.' This rejection can happen to people as well as things: 'Ah said Ah'd gie her a lift hame but she knocked us back.' 'How d'ye no ask her oot? She's no gauny knock ye back.'

An instance of this is a **knockback**: 'Ah hear she applied fur that joab but goat a knockback.' 'Cheer up, son . . . never hud a knockback fae a lassie before?'

knot **To knot yourself** is to laugh enthusiastically: 'Ye'll knot yersel when ye hear this yin!' 'We were pure knottin wursels at his daft patter.'

K.P. An abbreviation and nickname for the Kinning Park area of the South Side: 'Jeanie, here a couple from the K.P. that knew your mother.'

The pair a them wis lummed up before they even got tae the reception.

laldy An odd word, basically denoting vigour, whether applied to punishment or enthusiastic participation. To **give it laldy** means to give one's utmost enthusiasm and effort to whatever it is one is doing: 'The boy wi the Lambeg drum wisny hauf giein it laldy.' To **give someone laldy** is to give the person a severe chastisement, whether physically or verbally: 'Aye, yer granda used ta gie us laldy wi a slipper fur the likes a that.'

Lally's Palais *or* **The Lally Palais** A nickname for the Royal Concert Hall, at the head of Buchanan Street, from its being planned and built while Pat Lally (later Lord Provost) was head of the City Council.

lamp To **lamp** someone is to hit him: 'He just walked up tae the big diddy an lampt him wan in the mooth.' It can also mean to throw something: 'That's the guy that lamped a half-brick at the polis.'

Lanny A nickname for Lanliq, a proprietary brand of fortified wine: 'Gie um a boatle a Lanny an that'll be him happy.'

lavvy A toilet, shortened from *lavatory*: 'Aw naw! Ma wallies've went doon the lavvy pan!' Someone whose hair has been cut short so that it stands up may be said to have **a heid like a lavvy brush**.

A plumber is sometimes referred to disrespectfully as a **lavvy-diver**: 'Ah'm no puttin ma haun doon there. That's a joab fur a lavvy-diver.'

lay it off To talk about something at great length and with an air of imparting important information: 'Ah wish she wid stoap layin it aff tae us aboot gaun tae Uni.'

leader-off The person who takes the initiative in an activity, whether it be an innocent pastime like singing, or as the leader of a gang: 'I might have known you'd be the leader-off in this carry-on.'

left-footer *or* **left-fitter** A slang word for a Roman Catholic: 'They're aw left-fitters in that department.'

lend *or* **len** A loan: 'See's a len a yer ladders, will ye?' To **take a len** or **loan** of a person is to exploit him without him knowing it, often in a manner that makes him look gullible and credulous: 'Ye'd think he'd learn a lesson seein the right len a him she took the last time.'

length **To go the length of** means to travel as far as: 'We're no gaun the length o Paisley but we could drap ye at the Haufway.'

Someone who is seen as being very lazy may have it said of him that he **wouldny walk the length of himself**.

Light Blues, the A nickname for Rangers F.C., from the colour of their jerseys.

like that The phrase **I was like that** (or she was, we were, etc) often crops up in a conversational narration, meaning the speaker was surprised, shocked, dumbfounded, etc, depending on the context. Obviously it is meant to be accompanied by a pantomime of the relevant facial expression or bodily stance, but it is commonly used without any such visual aid (even on the phone) and can be described as mere verbal padding: 'She says "You're no comin wae us" an Ah wis lik that. Ah says "How've Ah no tae get?" and she wis lik that, an she says . . .'

line A **line** or **bookie's line** is a betting slip or the actual bet itself: 'Ah'll maybe nip doon an put a wee line on.' 'This line's beat.' 'He says he's left the line in his ither jaiket.'

Another type of line is a **sick line** or **doctor's line**, a certificate from a GP attesting to a sick employee's unfitness for work: 'Yer self-certificate's ran oot. Ye'll need tae get a line fae the doctor.'

Some shops or stores operate a discount facility for staff, and a person for whom this is available is often said to have **a line for** that particular store: 'Her next door's got a line for Marks.'

Lipton's orphan A proverbial poor-looking person: 'Ah tried on your coat but it wis far too big fur us. Ah looked lik Lipton's orphan in it.' This comes from a well-known advertising poster produced by Lipton the Grocer in which a man is shown carrying a pig, which is clearly unhappy and crying, in a sack on his back. A lady is asking him what's wrong with the pig, and his reply is that it's an orphan and the rest of the family have gone to Lipton's.

Lisbon Lions, the The nickname for the famous Celtic F.C. team who, in Lisbon in 1967, became the first British side to win the European Cup: 'Sure Wee Jinky wis wan a the Lisbon Lions, Da?'

live up with A common phrase meaning to live in sin, cohabit with someone to whom you are not married: 'Aye, that's him that left his wife an weans tae live up wi some floozy fae Partick.'

loaded A descriptive term meaning full of the cold, having a runny nose, sore head, etc: 'Aw ya poor wee soul, ye're loaded. Away hame tae yer bed wi a hot toddy.'

Lodge, the Sometimes pronounced *ludge*, only one kind of lodge is understood by this, i.e. the Orange Lodge: 'Whit d'ye make a that referee . . . another wan up for the Lodge, eh?'

'lok A nickname for Pollok F.C., a well-supported Junior side based at Newlandsfield on the South Side: ''lok hopes dashed in penalty shootout.'

long The expression **as long** means an unspecified but lengthy time: 'Her wean's picture wis in that photographer's windae for as long.' **Long enough** similarly means a long period: 'If he makes a baws ae it this time he'll wait long enough for another chance.'

The phrase **a long road for a short cut** is used when what is intended to be a quicker route to travel or a faster way of doing something seems to take longer than the usual way: 'I know it looks like a long road for a short cut but it works out quicker in the end.'

looked The unusual construction **get your head looked** is a local way of referring to a psychiatric examination: 'Ye said naw tae an offer lik that? You need tae get yer heid looked, pal!'

loop *or* **loop-de-loop** A crazy person: 'Ah canny believe you're hingin aboot wi a loop lik that.'

loosie A slang word for a cigarette sold individually in a shop, as bought by those who are short of funds or underage: 'This guy'll sell ye a loosie nae bother, on ye go.'

Lorne sausage Also known as **square sausage**, this is sausage meat shaped into oblong blocks before being cut into slices: 'Away roon tae the butcher's for a half-pun a Lorne sausage an a couple a slices a beef ham.' Apparently the 'Lorne' name comes from the Glasgow comedian Tommy Lorne (1890-1935) who was not enamoured of the delicacy, comparing such slices to doormats.

loss This is often used as a verb, meaning to *lose*: 'Ah'm gauny loss the heid if this cairries on!'

loupin From a Scots word meaning *jump*, this is used to mean extremely painful: 'Ah bet yer heid's loupin efter last night.'

It can also mean infested (as in, 'Look at that wean clawin her heid. She must be loupin.') or very busy with, full of: 'The toon's loupin wi Welsh rugby supporters.'

low-flyer A nickname for a measure of The Famous Grouse, a popular proprietary brand of whisky (from the behaviour of the bird).

luckies A nicely apt word for things of value found in rubbish bins, as hunted by midgie-rakers: 'Ah went doon wi the rubbish an fun an aul dosser gaun through the bins fur luckies.'

lucky bag A bag containing sweets and a cheap toy or gift, as bought by children from sweetie shops. The point is that the purchaser doesn't know exactly what is in the bag until it is opened, and the term is often used to disparage something that the speaker doesn't think much of: 'Check his new mobey! Did ye get that in a lucky bag?'

lucky middens A slang term for household rubbish bins where substantial **luckies** are likely to be found. Also extended to describe an area where such middens are the norm: 'I hear you've moved to Newton Mearns. That's you up in the lucky middens now, eh?'

lumber **To get a lumber** is to meet and establish a relationship with a member of the opposite sex: 'How did ye get on at that party . . . did ye get a lumber?'

To lumber a person is to chat her or him up successfully: 'That guy you're hingin aboot wi wis tryin tae lumber us last night.'

lummed up A slang term for drunk: 'The pair a them wis lummed up before they even got tae the reception.'

Lum, of course, is a Scots word for chimney, but apart from seeing someone as reeking with the fumes of alcohol the connection between drunkenness and chimneys escapes me.

lumps To **kick lumps out of** someone is to give him a good hiding: 'It was the kind of boozer where if two punters start kickin lumps out of one another nobody bothers their backside.'

The image of his meat...

ma¹ A local version of *my*: 'Ma maw's a millionaire!'

ma² Also **mammy** or **maw**, one's mother: 'Couldny be better, Ma!' 'Ye canny shove yer Granny, cause she's yer Mammy's Mammy . . .' 'Haw Maw! Whit's fur ma tea?'

Many Glaswegians are particularly sensitive to insults to their mothers (apparently it's okay to slag fathers), and this has given rise to such barbs as **yer maw's a big man, yer maw's a brickie, yer mammy's a bun,** and so on.

Maccy, the A nickname for Maxwell Park, a public park on the South Side: 'Dae they still have boats on the Maccy pond?'

At one time it was said that you were not a fully-fledged Kinning-Parker until you had fallen into the Maxwell Park pond while hunting for baggies.

MacWhachle Wee MacWhachle is an affectionate nonsense name for any toddler: 'Wait till ye see Wee MacWhachle comin over when Ah rustle this bag a sweeties.'

maddy A crazy person: 'He wis shoutin an bawlin like a maddy.'

Someone who exhibits violent anger may be said to **take a maddy**: 'The parkie'll take a pure maddy if he sees ye pickin they flooers.'

mad skull A local term for an unstable or wild person: 'The way that bam drives, he should have a sticker in his back windy sayin "Mad Skull on Board".'

Maggie May, the A nickname for St Margaret Mary's Secondary School in Castlemilk.

malky Any cutting or stabbing weapon, especially (and originally) a cut-throat razor. To **get the malky** is to be physically attacked, not necessarily with a weapon: 'You're gauny get the malky if ye don't get aff yer mark.' This is used as a fairly vague threat, and is available in various degrees of harshness, from **the double malky** and **the treble malky** all the way up to **the severe malky**.

To **malky** a person is to attack him, especially using a bladed weapon: 'Tell the crapbag Big Ronnie's on his way roon tae malky him.' 'They brung a boay inty Casualty that'd been malkied. Blood aw ower the shoap!'

To **get malkied in** is to do something with great vigour and enthusiasm.

The term seems to have originated as the first half of a piece of Glasgow rhyming slang: Malky (a common shortening of Malcolm) Fraser, meaning *razor*. My researches have failed to identify the Malcolm Fraser thus commemorated.

mark To scar, used as a threat: 'Get oot ma road afore Ah mark ye.'

masel Myself: 'Ah'm a fool tae masel, so Ah am.'

mate aboot To associate with someone as friends, have a particular person as your best pal: 'Yer faither an me used tae mate aboot thegither when we were in John Brown's yard.'

meat Used in the sense of food in general (not just cooked animals) this turns up in the phrase **it's your meat that makes ye bonny**. It is often said of a child that is plump and healthy, well-fed looking, that he is **the image of his meat**.

mee-maws A nickname for the police, imitating the sound of a squad car's siren: 'Ah got wakened up in the middle a the night wi the mee-maws fleein doon the street.'

There's the old joke about the proud mother who has three strapping sons in the police force. Towards the end of their dinner she asks 'Who's fur merr puddin?' and hears in reply 'Me Maw, me Maw, me Maw!'

melt To **melt** a person is to strike him powerfully: 'He jumped ower the table an meltit him wan.' This comes from the earlier Scots use of the term to mean to hit someone in the region of the *melt* or spleen.

The phrase **get inty his melt** is used to encourage another person to attack a third party or, if a fight is already in progress, to put more effort into it: 'Are you gauny take that crap aff the likes a him? Get inty his melt!'

mental To **go mental** is to lose your temper in a big way: 'She'll go pure mental when she sees that phone bill!'

Someone who is wild, unstable, or given to extravagant losses of temper may be called a **mental** or a **mental case**: 'A gang a mentals got on the bus an widny pay their ferr.'

Mentalness is the state of being crazy or a display of this: 'What's gaun on in there the day is nothin but pure mentalness.'

mentions When a youth is scrawling grafitti on a wall or other surface and one of his mates wants to be named in the roll of honour he will be told 'Gie's mentions.'

This is sometimes shortened to **mensh** or **menshies**: 'How'd ye no gie me an Hammy menshies?'

mere A local form of *come here*, shortened in speech from the already compressed *c'mere*: 'Mere you! Whit's this you're sayin aboot me?'

merrit Married: 'She's merrit ontae wan a they McLaffertys fae Smith Street.'

mess To **mess** is to interfere, to get involved with somebody else's business, especially in a way likely to cause a fight (whether intentionally or not): 'Are you messin wi me, pal?' 'Ye don't mess wi the best.'

Someone who causes trouble in this way (or simply anyone who makes a mess) may be called a **messer**: 'That wee messer's just stirrin it.'

message To go for the messages or do the messages means to do the shopping. The items bought are known as **messages**: 'Wis that you Ah saw staggerin up the road wi a ton a messages?' A shopping bag is often referred to as a **message bag**. Any kind of errand, not necessarily to buy something, may be called a **message**: 'She'll be back in a minute: she's just away a wee message.'

To **give someone the message** is to convince him of the error of his ways, either by verbal chastisement or the use of physical force: 'Boy, Ah'll gie you the message all right if Ah catch ye at this wee gemme again.'

messin A mildly abusive name, particularly used for naughty children. 'He's et the hale packet, the greedy wee messin!' The word originally meant a small dog.

mibby A local form of *maybe*: 'That'll mibby teach her a lesson.' Some people, especially older Glaswegians, also say **mibbies**: 'Mibbies aye, mibbies naw.'

Mick's blood A slang term for Guinness.

midden This can mean a dustbin or the area behind a tenement block where the dustbins are kept. It is also applied to people or places considered slovely or unclean: 'The dirty aul midden hasny had a bath fur months.' 'Get this midden of a room tidied up right now.'

midgie Another word for **midden**: 'There's a deid cat lyin in the midgie.' A **midgie-bin** is a dustbin, which is likely to be emptied by a **midgie-man** (dustman) into a **midgie-motor** (bin lorry). Someone who, for one reason or another, searches rubbish bins for things of value or use may be called a **midgie-raker**.

Milk *or* **Mulk, the** A familiar name for the Castlemilk area in

107

the south of the city: 'We're meetin up wi a couple a boys fae the Mulk.' In recognition of this, a local paper is called *The Milk Round*.

millions A substantial quantity (rather than number) of anything: 'He flung that can in the bin an there wis millions left in it!'

mince For some reason the name of this traditional filling for pies or accompaniment for totties has been borrowed by the dialect for a variety of meanings.

It can mean nonsense or deliberate untruthfulness: 'That's total mince you're talkin.' 'Do they expect us to believe this mince?' Another meaning is that of anything nasty or dirty: 'What's this mince on the sleeve of my coat?'

Mincey is an adjective formed from this, meaning of inferior quality or contemptible: 'Ah want tae watch the gemme oan a big plasma screen, no a mincey wee telly lik that.'

It is taken as a measure of density, whether of the brain or another substance: 'Is he no very bright? The guy's as thick as mince!' Some people refer to a pint of Guinness as a **pint of mince**. A person who seems to be very quiet, listless or downcast may be told they are **sittin there like a pun a mince**.

To **sicken someone's mince** is to spoil something for him or deflate him: 'It didny hauf sicken his mince when he didny get that bonus.' To **get inty someone's mince** is to attack them physically: 'Beat it afore Ah get right inty your mince, bawbag!'

minder A small gift, often bought as a thank-you token for someone who has done you a kindness: 'She's been a right good neighbour over the years. I'll need to get her a wee minder before we go.'

mines A variation of *mine*: 'He's already et his dinner an now he's wantin mines!'

ming Anything that smells unpleasant may be said **to ming**: 'That cheese disny hauf ming.' **A ming** is a stink: 'See the ming when Ah took the lid aff the bin?'

108

Mingin means unpleasantly smelly: 'Sumdy's feet are mingin in here.' Its use is extended to cover anything that is considered bad or contemptible: 'Ah wis that lookin forward tae that film an it turned oot tae be mingin.' 'That shirt's a pure mingin colour.' It can also mean drunk: 'By the time Ah got there they were aw mingin an Ah jist went hame.'

A minger (rhymes with *singer*) is anything that is smelly, dirty or otherwise objectionable: 'Their new single's a total minger.' 'She thinks she's hot but she's a pure minger.'

Some of these usages (*minging* and *minger* in particular) have spread to youth culture in other parts of Britain, but it was in Glasgow that they first became current.

minkin This may well be a variation of **mingin**; it certainly covers a similar range of meanings, especially extremely smelly or otherwise unpleasant: 'Sumdy open a windy. It's pure minkin in here.' Someone who exhibits these qualities can be described as a **minker**.

minted A slang term used to describe anything you approve of or think is excellent: 'Ah hear ye passed yer test. That's minted, wee man!' Perhaps this derives from the idea of a brand-new shiny coin, freshly minted, that stands out from the other dull coins in your change.

It is also used to mean wealthy: 'Have ye seen their motor? They must be minted!'

miraculous (usually pronounced *marockyoolus*) this means extremely drunk. It has been around a long time, as shown by this 1873 extract from the former Glasgow periodical *The Bailie*, in which a court witness was asked to describe the degree of drunkenness exhibited by an accused person: 'I've seen him the waur o' whusky; he had got a dram, an' was a little intoxicated, but he wasna miraklous.'

The term is sometimes shortened to **maroc**: 'Did ye see the nick a her last night? Maroc or what?'

miss **To miss yourself** is not to somehow become aware of the absence of your own body, but to fail to experience something enjoyable through not being in the right place at the right time: 'Ye missed yersel, no comin on Saturday . . . it wis a rerr night.'

If you are angry with someone and are telling a third party exactly what you will do when you catch up with the offender, you might say **Ah'll no miss him** or, in its fuller form, **Ah'll no miss him an hit the waw**.

mix, the Someone who deliberately sets out to cause trouble between two other parties may be said to **put the mix in**: 'Never mind what the wee ratbag says, he's just tryin tae put the mix in.' An alternative version of this is **the mixy**.

moan A shortened form of *c'moan*, come on: 'Ye comin or no? Moan then!'

mobbed Crowded with people: 'Ye couldny get near the shops. They were aw mobbed.'

mockit *or* **mawkit** This can mean soiled or dirty: 'Ye're no gaun oot in they mockit troosers, are ye?' It is also used to mean dirty in the sense of obscene or lewd: 'How come ye never actually see anybody takin oot wan a they mockit DVDs?' **Mockitness** is the state of being mockit, or an example of this: 'Somethin'll need tae be done aboot the general mockitness of this kitchen.'

model A hostel or lodging-house for single homeless people: 'Ye're gaun aboot lik somethin oot a model.' A **modeller** in this case is someone who lives in a model. The term comes from the more formal Model Lodging House, the original title of many such establishments.

mollocate To beat up or thrash: 'The aul man'll mollocate ye if he gets ye.'

Monday Book A common nickname for a book of DSS benefit vouchers, so called because the vouchers are all dated to become payable on Mondays: 'The wean wis playin wi ma Monday book an noo Ah'm gaun mental lookin fur it.'

monty A slang expression meaning hurry up or don't be silly: 'Where is that eejit? Here you! Monty!' This is a shortening

110

of one or two similar phrases, the least offensive being **monty grips**, which literally means come to grips.

moolly A term used to describe someone considered mean or miserly: 'The moolly aul get never gied us a bung.'

moony A slang word for a slow embracing dance, or the music for it, most commonly observed at the end of a disco when the romantic tracks are played: 'Ah'm that shy Ah hide in the lavvy when a moony comes oan.'

moose's meat A nickname, fairly contemptuous, for cheese: 'Ah could never be a vegetarian. Ah need more tae keep me gaun than moose's meat an rabbit fodder.'

mooth The mouth. Someone considered to be well-endowed in this department may have it said of him that he has **a mooth like the Clyde Tunnel**. A person who has irregular or stained teeth may be described as having **a mooth like a row a condemned buildins** or **hooses**.

One of the unpleasant after effects of a heavy drinking session, especially when mixed with smoking, is **a mooth like a pocketful a douts**. A similar expression is **a mooth like a badger's erse** or **bum**. One can't help but wonder why a badger should be considered particularly unpleasant in this department and, indeed, how anyone found out.

A **moothful a heidies** is what is suffered by someone who is head-butted: 'You wantin a moothful a heidies, pal?' Another version of this is **a moothful a dandruff**.

The phrase **you've a mooth** indicates an offer of food or drink to a guest: 'D'ye know Ah sat in that hoose fur a good oor an a hauf an they never thought to say "You've a mooth"!'

moothie A mouth-organ or harmonica: 'Her aul boy's a dab hand at the moothie.'

morra, the A local version of *the morrow*, that is, tomorrow: 'Ah'll be away the day, the night an the morra.' 'At this rate ye'll no be finished till the bliddy morra!' **The morra night** is tomorrow night: 'It's no the night it's oan, it's the morra night.'

mortalled Another word for drunk, a local variant of the Scots term *mortal*: 'He tries tae tell us he only had wan or two. Away, Ah says, mortalled wisny in it!'

Mount, the A familiar name for the Mount Florida area on the South Side: 'Ah liked it when we stayed up in the Mount. It wis a real wee community.'

movin Moving, a descriptive adjective meaning infested with lice, presumably so badly that you can see them moving around: 'Ah'd tae sit next tae this poor wee soul at the doactor's. Nae jaiket nor nothin, an his heid wis movin.'

Muldoon's picnic A term used for a social event which seems rather chaotic, such as when a miscellaneous group of people sit down to a disorganised meal: 'I wouldn't exactly call it a dinner party. It was more like Muldoon's picnic.' The origin of the phrase is the title of a famous music-hall skit featuring the social misadventures of a drunken Irishman.

mully A slang term for emulsion paint: 'Slap another coat a mully oan it an that'll be us.'

Sampson was a strongman,
he lived on fish an chips.
He went along the Galloway te
pickin up the nips

-nae *or* **-ny** Literally meaning *not*, this is a negative suffix common enough in Scots, as in *cannae, willny,* etc. It is used on its own by local children to contradict the last thing said to them, as if immediately adding the negative to a word the speaker has used: 'Right! You're comin hame this minute!' '-Nae!' 'Ye are so!' '-Nae!' This kind of argument is not only maddening but invincible if persisted with, as there is nothing you can say that can't be thus negated. You either give up or resort to nonverbal measures.

naebdy *or* **noabdy** Two local variants of *nobody*: 'Naebdy came tae the door.' 'Noabdy wantin these spiced onions?'

nae nae kiddin Definitely no kidding, an emphatic insistence that you are telling the truth, used especially by children. It can also be used as a question, meaning you're not having me on, are you?: 'Look, Ah'll definitely get ye in fur nothin.' 'Nae nae kiddin?' 'Nae nae kiddin.'

nae tother This means no trouble: 'We'll get this finished the

113

morra nae tother.' It's shortened from *nae tother a baw*, which is a deliberately spoonerised version of *nae bother at aw*.

naw A local version of *no*: 'Aw naw! Ma galluses've snapped!'

neb Another word for *nose*: 'Just you keep yer aul neb out of this.' It is also used to mean a nosey (also, sometimes, cheeky) individual: 'What wis that wee neb askin ye?' **A neb** can also be an instance of being nosey or prying: 'Is she no back from the toilet yet? She must be havin a neb round upstairs.'

   To neb is to pry into matter that don't concern you, be inquisitive: 'Tell him to mind his own business instead of comin round here nebbin.'

neck To **get** or **take a red neck** is to be embarrassed to the point of blushing: 'Ah get a red neck every time that wean opens his mooth.'

   In a bar, if a customer asks for a bottle of beer **by the neck** this means he doesn't want it poured into a glass, either because he intends to use a glass he already has or he means to drink straight from the bottle: 'Gie's two pints a seventy an a Sol by the neck.'

   To **go on your neck** means to fall heavily, especially flat on your back: 'She walked onty the wet flerr an went on her neck, the soul.'

ned A hooligan or criminal, usually young, or someone who acts or dresses like one: 'I'm fed up getting cheek from these neds that loiter outside the chip shop.' The word can also be an adjective: 'This is pure ned behaviour.' 'She's got a right ned face on her.' Something that seems suitable for or typical of neds can be described as **neddy**: 'You won't catch me in a neddy boozer like that!' 'Check his neddy wee baseball hat.'

   Some people are convinced that ned is an abbreviation for 'Non-Educated Delinquent', but this is merely wishful thinking. The word ned was in use as long ago as the 1950s, long before the late-20th-century craze for abbreviations and acronyms, and was derived from the man's name *Edward*, in much the same way as 'Teddy-boy'.

114

neebur A **neebur** is a neighbour, and can also mean specifically a person who works beside or with you: 'Your uncle wis ma neebur in Butters years ago.' The word often appears as a term of address for someone you feel friendly towards: 'How ye getting on, neebur? Hinging thegither?' **Neebs** is a shortened form of this: 'Aw right, neebs?'

needle To **take the needle** is to take offence: 'We wur just muckin aboot. There wis nae need fur him tae take the needle.'

neither Used in forming additional reinforcing remarks at the end of a negative statement: 'He'll no get away the day, neither he will.' The opposite of this is **so**.

newp When decimal curency was introduced in the early 1970s everything was counted in new pence, which was immediately and typically shortened to **newps**. Although no longer current in everyday use you will still hear the word in certain fixed contexts, such as a twenty-pence piece being called **twenty newps**: 'Any a youse goat twinty newps fur this meter?'

new start An employee who has only recently joined a firm, often the butt of wicked japes: 'Right, whit wan a youse comedians sent the new start fur a tin a tartan paint?'

nick¹ To **nick** is to go somewhere quickly or briefly: 'He's nicked oot fur a fag.' The phrase **nick about** has several meanings. It can mean to circulate in a particular area: 'He's always nickin aboot the shoppin centre on a Saturday.' It is also used to refer to someone who has an active social life and is often seen around and about places of entertainment: 'She fairly nicks about, that yin.' To **nick about with** means to frequent the company of: 'He's just a guy Ah nick aboot wi.'

nick² The **nick** of something or someone is the condition it or he is in. If a person is looking the worse for wear someone might comment: 'Some nick, eh?' A person wishing to draw another's attention to a state that is worthy of comment may invite them to **check the nick of that**.

115

nineteen-canteen An imaginary date long ago, time immemorial: 'Ah've no been doon the watter since nineteen-canteen!' Another version of this is **nineteen-oatcake**.

nip To **nip** is to be sore: 'Gie's an aspreen or somethin . . . ma heid's nippin!' It can also mean to hurt: 'These new shoes're nippin ma feet somethin rotten.' To **nip someone's heid** is to perpetually nag or upbraid him: 'Gauny gie it a rest, nippin ma heid aboot that washin-machine?'

To **nip** a person can mean to pick him or her up, to meet and establish a relationship with him or her: 'Ah'm gaun oot tae see if Ah kin nip a wee burd the night.' 'Hey you! Ma pal says she wants tae nip you!'

The expression is also used to mean to borrow money: 'Ah'll see if Ah kin nip the brother fur a ten-spot.' Someone who is trying to secure such a loan is described as being **at the nip**: 'Kid on ye don't see him. He'll be at the nip, sure as guns.' A person who gets a reputation for always trying to borrow money may find that he is labelled by this habit: 'Don't tell us ye lent money tae Jimmy the Nip!'

To **nip** a cigarette is to put it out by pinching the lit end between the fingers, usually with a view to smoking the remainder later on: 'It started rainin, so Ah'd tae nip ma fag an stick it behind ma ear.'

A **nip** can mean a partly-smoked cigarette that has been pinched out in this way or simply a cigarette-end thrown away, as commemorated in the following delightful traditional rhyme:

Samson was a strongman,
He lived on fish an chips.
He went along the Gallowgate,
Pickin up the nips.

nippie A brief or quick excursion: 'We'll do a wee nippie inty the bookie's on the way back.'

nippy sweetie The original meaning of this is a boiled sweet that has a sour flavour or makes the mouth feel hot. It is most commonly used now to mean a drink of spirits: 'Ah've no got time fur a pint, but if ye put ma arm up ma back Ah'll mibby manage a quick nippy sweetie.'

It can also mean a person with a short temper or a sour disposition: 'He can be a bit of a nippy sweetie if ye rub him up the wrong way, but he's no a bad guy really.'

Nitsie, the A nickname for Nitshill, a housing scheme on the South Side: 'It's gauny be some night ... the boys fae the Nitsie are aw comin.'

Noddytown A nickname for Cumbernauld, partly from the -*nauld* element of the 'new' town's name, and partly because it doesn't seem like a 'real' town to many Glaswegians. So, next time they ask you what it's called, you'll know.

noise To **noise up** a person is to deliberately provoke or irritate them: 'Dae Ah get the impression you're tryin tae noise me up, shorty?'

This seems to have originated as a motoring term, meaning to sit behind another car at a red traffic light, revving your engine in an intimidatory manner.

Nollie *or* **Nolly, the** A local nickname for the Forth and Clyde Canal, which passes through the north of the city: 'Ah huvny hud so much fun since Ah used tae go ferret-racin on the Nollie banks.'

This comes from a shortening of the local pronunciation of canal as *ca-nawl*. The canal is spanned by a bridge known as the **Nolly Brig** and sailed by a pleasure craft known as the **Nolly Barge**.

noo *or* **now, the** This is the common Scots from of *now*. In Glasgow speech an intrusive *s* can be heard, creating such variants as **s'now, isnow,** and even **the snow**: 'Are we gaun isnow?' It's almost as if it was 'this now' (as opposed to any other now) which is being said, but it may be more to do with a contraction of *just now*.

nood book A slang term for a pornographic magazine: 'Miss! He's got a nood book under his desk!' The local use of *book* to mean 'magazine' is also shown by the fact that a *dirty book* can be a porno mag as well as a sexy novel.

no real Literally, not real, this is used to mean outrageous, insane, unbelievable, and so on: 'Did ye hear that wee bampot diggin up the Big Man? The boay's pure no real!'

nosey To **do one's nosey** is to act inquisitively, look around a place in an intrusive, prying way: 'Have you got nothin better to do than come round here doin yer nosey?'

note A slang term for a pound (sterling): 'It's gauny cost ye fifty notes.' The reference is, of course, to £1 notes, which are used in Scotland despite being phased out in other parts of the United Kingdom.

nougat (pronounced *nugget*) A wafer filled with mock cream and coated with chocolate, as served with ice cream. A **single nougat** consists of one of these with a slab of ice cream sandwiched between it and a plain wafer. For real gannets, a **double nougat** is the same thing but with the plain wafer replaced by another nougat.

no-user (the second part rhymes with *juicer*) A contemptuous term for a good-for-nothing or shiftless individual: 'Ah'd hate tae see ye turn oot a big no-user like yer auld man, son.'

nuchin Pronounced with the *ch* as in *loch*, this is a local variant of *nothing*, popular perhaps because the *ch* sound lends it added vehemence: 'An what dae Ah get out a this? Nuchin!'

nugget A slang term for a one-pound coin: 'Ah hate havin a pocket full a nuggets. It pure ruins the line a yer strides.'

nuhin Another variant of *nothing* in broad Glaswegian speech: 'There nuhin left.'

numpty An idiot: 'See you? Ye're a grade-wan numpty, flyin colours, nae resits!'

nut A version of *no*, most often used on its own in reply to a question: 'Ah asked him if he wis comin oot fur a dauner an aw he said wis "Nut".'

nyaff A disparaging term for a despicable or irritating person, especially one small in stature: 'Tell that wee nyaff Ah'm gauny boot his arse fae here tae Govan.' The word seems to derive from an older Scots term for the bark of a little dog.

Interestingly enough though, Partridge's *Dictionary of Slang* refers to a Parisian slang word *gniaffe* (a term of abuse for a man) which would have a similar pronunciation. Perhaps the Académie Française would cite this as an example of the Auld Alliance corrupting the French language.

nyuck A disparaging term for anyone you dislike, for whatever reason: 'That wis a right shower a nyucks sittin in fronty us at the ballet last night.'

An oyster fur yer granda.

oary boat A local term for a rowing boat: 'Sure Bonnie Prince Charlie went tae Skye in an oary boat? Ah seen it oan the telly.'

off The phrase **for the off** has several meanings:

1. about to leave, departing: 'Is that you for the off? Ah'll see ye doon the road.'

2. being dismissed from a job: 'Ah hear there's five ae us fur the off.'

3. about to die: 'Wan merr fright like yon an Ah'll be fur the off.'

offie A familiar term for an off-licence: 'Does that offie do lottery tickets as well?'

offski A slang way of saying *off*, as in departing: 'Wan merr cup a coffee an Ah'm offski.'

old *or* **auld** Used in various combinations meaning *father*. **old boy, old man, old fella. Old yin** can be mother or father. **Old dear, old doll, old girl** all mean *mother*. 'Tell yer auld dear wee Mrs Brannigan wis askin fur her.'

Old Firm, the A nickname for Celtic and Rangers football clubs when thought of together as institutional, traditional rivals: 'The Old Firm have been drawn together in the next round of the Cup.'

on To tell someone **you're not on** is to say there is no chance of your complying with his wishes: 'If ye think Ah'm gauny carry the can fur this baws-up ye're not on, sunbeam.'

onion bag A football journalists' cliché for the net of a goal: 'The boys in blue rattled three into the onion bag.'

ony *or* **olny** Two local versions of *only*: 'There's ony wan left an you're no getting it.'

oot scoot A phrase of dismissal, usually said to children who are in the speaker's way: 'Here, let me in that cupboard, weans. Oot scoot, beat it!'
    This probably comes from a children's game in which players are eliminated in turn by means of a chant ending 'oot scoot, you're oot.'

ooyah! A cry of pain, obviously just stopping short of calling 'you' something unprintable: 'Is that pie too hot yet? Ooyah!'

opposed A verbal distortion of *supposed* in the sense 'meant': 'Ye're no opposed tae park here, so ye're no.'

outsider Not a social outcast but any of the two thicker, often crustier, end slices of a loaf of bread: 'D'ye want this ootsider on yer piece?'

over it A local shortening of the common phrase 'over the moon' meaning delighted: 'Ah wis pure over it when Ah heard.'

ovies A familiar abbreviation of overalls: 'Aw Maw! Ye never washed ma ovies fur us!'

oyster A mouth-stretching delicacy obtainable from ice-cream sellers, consisting of two round shallow containers (like the two halves of an oyster shell) made of the same stuff as wafers.

One half is filled with ice cream and the other is placed on top to seal it. As this is far from being enough for the infamous Glasgow sweet tooth, one of the half-shells already contains a portion of artificial cream and is partly coated with coconut-sprinkled chocolate: 'Run out to the icey an get us aw a pokey-hat – an ye better get an oyster fur yer granda.'

A bum like a peemet...

P45 This, of course, is the official form given to an employee by an employer who is sacking him. In slang it is used when a person gets rid of a boyfriend or girlfriend: 'Ach him? Ah gied him his P45 last week.'

pa *or* **paw** Both used locally to mean *father*: 'Tell yer pa his tea's oot.' 'Could ye go another wee goldie, Paw?'

Paddy's Market The well-known street market, just off The Briggait, which gained its name through being frequented by impecunious Irish immigrants. Its rough-and-ready appearance and the miscellaneous nature of the goods on offer (everything from a secondhand wean's cardigan to a genuine Charles Rennie Mackintosh fireplace) ensured its use as a yardstick of untidiness: 'He's got the hoose lik Paddy's market since she went inty the hospital.'

Paisley The phrase **get off at Paisley** means to practise *coitus interruptus*. 'He said it wis awright, he wid get aff at Paisley, an now look at us!' This idea of 'not going all the way' is based on a train journey back to Glasgow from the Clyde Coast, Paisley being the last stop before Glasgow Central.

A **Paisley screwdriver** is a jocular term for a hammer, implying, in the way of these near-neighbourly rivalries, that the Paisley 'buddies' are none too bright.

pally ally (rhyming with *Sally*) A nickname for pale ale, being a deliberate mispronunciation of the words: 'If the exports are Phil's an the lagers are Irene's, whose are the pally allies?'

pamp To pamp the horn of a motor car is to blow it: 'Ah hate these folk that think they have tae pamp their horn when they're gaun away.' **A pamp** is an instance of doing this: 'He said tae wait ootside an gie the horn a wee pamp.'

pan To pan something is to burst it or break it: 'Sumdy's panned the chippie's windy in.' It can also mean to damage something deliberately and systematically, as for example breaking all the lights and windows of a car: 'The moneylender sent two guys roon wi hammers tae pan his motor.'

To **pan someone's melt in** is to give him a severe beating. Someone who works very hard at a task is said to **knock his pan in**: 'They pay ye buttons an expect ye tae knock yer pan in.'

panel A person who is unfit for work through illness and has been certified as such by a GP (i.e. given a **panel line**) may be said to be **on the panel**: 'He's been on the panel aw week an he's climbin the waws.' The original meaning of the phrase was that a person had been accepted onto a doctor's *panel* of patients who were treated free of charge.

panhandler A slang term for someone who is always scrounging, attempting to borrow money or goods: 'Ye're that saft, ye haun oot money tae any aul panhandler that asks ye.'

pan loaf This kind of bread, having a light crust all round it, gave its name to a posh way of speaking: **a pan-loaf accent**. Some say this is because pan loaves were more expensive than plain loaves; others explain it by suggesting that *pan loaf* is Glasgow rhyming slang for *toff* (pronounced *toaff*).

Pan-loafy is an adjective formed from this: 'She had yon kinna pan-loafy way a speakin.'

124

Pansy Potter A nickname bestowed on any female who performs a task requiring some physical strength: 'Look at Pansy Potter humphin they cases up the sterr herself!' This comes from the children's comic character 'Pansy Potter, the Strongman's Daughter' who was famous for feats of strength, originally in *The Beano*.

See also **Pansy Potters** under Rhyming slang.

pants Used in slang to mean:

1. rubbish, no good: 'Have ye heard their latest wan? It's pure pants, man!'

2. very easy, no bother: 'There's nothin tae it . . . it's a skoosh . . . it's pants!'

pap[1] This is used as a verb to mean *throw*. 'He papped a snowball at a polis motor.' Similarly, **pap out** means *throw out*: 'She went tae Strathclyde Uni but she got papped oot after a year.'

pap[2] A fool or soft character: 'Imagine a lassie a mines gaun aboot wi a pap lik yon.' The word originally meant a woman's breast or nipple and has thus been adapted in the same way as *diddy*.

papa Another name for a grandfather: 'See if yer papa wants another cup a tea.' Sometimes the grandsire's name is added, to avoid confusion if more than one is still to the fore: 'It's no Papa Ronnie that's takin ye; it's Papa John.'

pape Shortened from *papist*, this is a fairly offensive term for a Roman Catholic.

Paradise A nickname used among Celtic supporters for their home ground at Parkhead.

paralytic Often pronounced *paralettic*, this means extremely drunk: 'He disny think he's hud a good night if he disny end up paralettic.'

Parkhead Also known as Celtic Park, this is the home ground of Celtic F.C.: 'Ah hear they've ordered a bigger biscuit tin up at Parkheid.'

parkie A familiar term for a park-keeper: 'Ask the parkie what time they shut the gates.'

Parly Road A familiar name for Parliamentary Road, in the city centre: 'Her man got knocked doon wi a blue bus in Parly Road the other week.'

Partick The name of this district on the north-west side of the Clyde is found in the proverbial phrase **before the Lord left Partick**, meaning a very long time ago: 'Her faimly's stayed up this close since before the Lord left Partick. We're in this buildin twinty year an we're still the new folk tae her.'

Why Partick should be singled out as God-forsaken I cannot say, unless it has something to do with the area's high density of Glasgow University students.

party song Not a piece of musical jollification but an anthem of sectarian bigotry, as most often performed by devotees of football teams that attract such supporters: 'Right youse! Wan merr a yer party songs an yeez're aw barred.'

patter Your **patter** is what you have to say for yourself. If someone asks you to **gie's aw yer patter** this is a friendly invitation to expound some chat or pass on any news.

The term can also mean things said to impress others or amuse them: 'The guy's got mair patter than a double-glazin salesman.' 'Wait till ye hear her brother's patter . . . ye'll knot yersel!' **The patter** is also used to mean the kind of specialist language known only to insiders: 'She knows aw the patter aboot the internet an aw that.'

Two phrases used to express contempt for the standard of someone's patter are: **yer patter's like watter** and **yer patter's like toothpaste . . . it comes oot a tube.**

To patter away means to have a friendly, relaxed conversation: 'Ah didny think they'd get on but the pair of them've been patterin away aw night.'

Someone who tries to impress others with his line of chat may be called a **patter-merchant**, and the term is also used for someone who thinks he's funny but isn't: 'Aye, very funny, patter-merchant!'

pawnies *or* **ponnies** A nickname for the card game of pontoon: 'Let me put it this way, pal ... if this was a game a pawnies you'd be burst.'

peever Another name for hopscotch or for the stone or flattened can kicked around in the game: 'Look at this: somebody's chalked out the beds for peever!'

pelmet Someone whose backside is regarded as sticking out somewhat may be said to sport **a bum like a pelmet.**

pelters Severe verbal abuse or criticism: 'The councillor was getting pelters at the meeting about the new motorway.' 'They're aw giein us pelters aboot this cairry-oan an it's goat hee-haw tae dae wi me!'

people The celebratory cry **We are the people!** is often heard from football fans, or some other self-contained group, when they want to give vent to their feelings of superiority over the mass of humankind.

petted lip A facial expression in which the lower lip sticks out, indicative of sulking: 'Look at the petted lip on her ... ye could hang out a washin on it!'

P.F., the An abbreviation and nickname combined for a Procurator Fiscal: 'Ah've goat tae keep ma heid doon till the P.F. gets aff ma back.'

photie A photograph: 'The first prize in the raffle's a signed photie of Daniel O'Donnell.'
  D'ye want a photie? is a belligerent question addressed to a person that the speaker feels has been staring at them.

piece A term that covers any sandwich or even a single slice of bread spread with something: 'The wean wants a piece an jam.' 'Ah'm fed up wi corned beef on ma pieces.' 'Who's et the last cheese piece?' If a child asks for a piece and the person asks finds there is only bread but nothing to put on it, the child may be offered a **piece an breid.** The diminutive form **piecie** may be used when talking to children: 'Want a wee piecie, hen?'

A piecebox *or* **piecetin** is a container in which a worker or school pupil carries their lunch: 'Aw naw! Ah'm away withoot ma piecebox!'

The phrase **put her on a piece an eat her** is a terribly unromantic suggestion often shouted at kissing couples, demonstrating local contempt and distrust for public displays of passion in which football and inebriation are not involved.

pig A cruel term used among males for an unattractive female: 'Hey, Sammy, that wis a pure pig ye were winchin the other night.' An even more extreme form is a **pig wi knickers**.

If males are on the hunt for talent and they assess the bar or club they are in as being disappointing in that respect they may dismiss the place as a **pigs' ballroom**.

pinger (rhymes with *singer*) A slang term for a microwave oven, from the noise it makes to announce that the set cooking period has ended: 'Just fire it inty the pinger an gie it five minutes.'

pint dish A slang term for a pint tumbler: 'Imagine drinkin Martini oot a pint dish. You've got nae class, huv ye, ya toerag?'

pish A local version of *piss*. Also used to mean rubbish, nonsense or something of inferior quality: 'See you? Ye talk a lot a pish.' 'Ah seen that fillum. It wis pish.' Similarly, **pishy** means not very good: 'He's watchin wan a they pishy programmes on MTV.'

Pished means drunk: 'How did Ah end up talkin tae you? Ah must be pished!'

To **rip the pish** out of someone is to make fun of him.

plab A nicely onomatopoeic word for a cow's dropping: 'Ever stepped on a big coo's plab wi sandals on? It gets aw in between yer toes.'

The term can also be used for other varieties of excrement: 'You're oot enjoyin yersel an Ah'm stuck in the hoose up tae the elbows in plabby nappies!'

place A person who becomes wildly and unrestrainedly angry may be said to **lose the place**: 'Chill out, big man . . . nae need tae lose the place, eh?'

Away a place is a delicate euphemism for *dead*: 'When Ah seen that lorry wisny gauny stoap Ah thought Ah wis away a place.' It can also be a polite way of saying that someone is in the toilet: 'She'll be back in a minute. She's just away a wee place.' The latter can also be expressed as **go a place**: 'Ah'll need to go a place before we leave.'

plank To plank something is to hide it somewhere: 'The doughheid planked his winnin lottery ticket an noo he canny find it.' Such a hiding-place, or the stuff hidden in it, is called **a plank**: 'Yer Granny's got ginger snaps in a wee plank just for youse.'

To plank something down is to set it down heavily: 'He planked his big bahookie doon on the settee an said that wis him fur the night.'

play Someone who **plays himself** is not starring in his own biopic but messing about, not getting anything useful done: 'It would help if yeez would stop playin yersels and dae some graftin.'

The phrase **Ah'm no playin (wi youse)** is often used by a petulant child withdrawing from a game and sometimes used jocularly by adults.

playpiece Any snack eaten by a child during school playtime, not necessarily (or even usually) a sandwich: 'Can Ah have a packet a crisps fur ma playpiece?'

pleckie A slang shortening of *plectrum*, i.e. a guitar pick: 'He's crackin up cause he's lost the souvenir pleckie he got aff Kinky Friedman.'

plenties In much the same way as **mibby** can become **mibbies**, **plenty** is often heard as **plenties**: 'It's no finished at aw. There plenties left.'

plook *or* **pluke** A **plook** is a pimple or spot, especially on the face: 'If ye don't shut it Ah'm gauny play dot-tae-dot wi yer plooks.' The term is also used as a contemptuous name: 'Ye don't take snash aff a plook lik him.'

To plook a pimple or spot is to squeeze it with the fingers until it bursts: 'It hud a big yella heid oan it till Ah plookt it.'

Plooky means pimply or covered in spots: 'He'd be no bad lookin if he wisny so plooky.' 'Lookin at that big plooky coupon wid pit ye aff yer dinner.'

plootered Yet another word meaning *drunk*: 'Just leave the tube where he is. Serves him right for getting plootered this early.' This may be connected with the Scots word *plowter* meaning splash or dip in liquid.

plums The phrase **you're onto plums** is used to tell someone that he has been unsuccessful or there is nothing doing: 'If ye think ye're getting a freebie aff me ye're onty plums, pal!' Why this pleasant fruit should be considered as second prize or undesirable I cannot tell. Some people substitute **a bag of plums** or **rice** as what you are onto.

plunge **To plunge** someone is to stab him: 'Mind that rammy ootside the kebab shoap last night? Ah hear a boay goat plunged.'

plunk A fairly old-fashioned word meaning to dodge school, play truant: 'Ah'd've got on better in life if Ah hadny plunked the school so much.' Someone who plays truant from school may be called a **plunker**.

pochle A **pochle** is any dishonest contest or business transaction: 'Aye, an yer Christmas draw's nothin but a pochle every year!'

To pochle something is to acquire it by means of a swindle or cheating, or to be responsible for a fraud: 'She got her books for pochlin her expenses.'

podger A slang term meaning to have sexual intercourse with: 'Aye, Ah'd podger that aw right!'

pokey-hat A local term for an ice-cream cone: 'Get yer granda doon tae the café an he'll maybe buy ye a pokey-hat.'

polis This can mean the police ('Ah'm gauny get the polis tae youse'), an individual police officer ('He's no a bad big guy . . . fur a polis'), or a number of police officers ('Ah seen him runnin doon the back lane wi two polis on his tail').

A police station is often referred to as a **polis office** (pronounced *oaffis*): 'Ah'm phonin the polis office if youse don't turn doon that racket.'

The word also turns up in the phrase **murder polis** which can either be an exclamation of consternation or shock ('Murder polis! The weans've broke ma washin line!') or a description of a difficult or confused situation ('It'll be murder polis gaun tae work the morra if they don't get these roads gritted').

Polomint City A nickname, which was originally coined by CB enthusiasts but which spread to wider use, for East Kilbride. This comes from the exceptional proliferation of roundabouts encountered when driving through it: 'He wis last heard of in Polomint City tryin tae get onty the Motherwell Road.'

Posso A familiar name for Possilpark, on the north side of the city, perhaps reflecting a local pronunciation of *Possil*: 'Wee Damien fae Posso.'

P.R., the A nickname and abbreviation for Paisley Road West, a main thoroughfare on the south-west bank of the Clyde: 'If ye get onty the P.R. any bus'll take ye inty toon.'

pretendy Originally used in children's games to denote anything made up for the purposes of play ('That hut's oor pretendy fort'), the word is often employed to disparagingly describe anything considered phoney: 'Mind big Connolly said Scotland had a pretendy Parliament?'

Priestie, the A nickname for the Priesthill area in the South Side: 'She got a cooncil flat in Priestie efter her man goat aff his mark.'

prod *or* **proddy** The word *protestant* is commonly pronounced *prodestant*, and these terms are shortenings of that: 'Are you a proddy dog or a catholic cat?' 'The proddies aw go tae that school.' 'Is that a Tim name or a Prod wan?'

Prosecutin Fiscal An alternative title for the Procurator Fiscal, commonly used among those who have cause to see his role in this light: 'Ah never done nothin. Ah'm complainin tae the Prosecutin Fiscal aboot this.'

Provvy cheque A slang term for a cheque issued by Provident Personal Credit Ltd: 'Evrubdy roon here gets their Christmas prezzies wi a Provvy cheque.'

This is a credit arrangement whereby someone borrows (at interest) a sum from this company, the funds being supplied as a cheque to be exchanged for goods at a shop that displays a sign indicating that it accepts such cheques.

puff candy A type of confection of a hard, crumbly consistency that tends, as I recall, to stick to the teeth (of which it is, no doubt, highly destructive). The term is used, especially by schoolkids, to mean easily done, no bother: 'That test was pure puff candy, Miss!' It is sometimes shortened to **puff**: 'C'mon, this'll be puff.'

puggled If a person is described as **puggled** this can mean he is slightly drunk, or just daft: 'Gie me that remote. You're too puggled tae use it.'

puggy This word turns up in various situations concerning money. It can be the kitty in a card game: 'The puggy's a fiver each, right?' **A puggy** can also be a one-armed bandit or other kind of gambling machine: 'It's no much fun goin for a pint wi a guy that just wants tae staun at that stupit puggy aw night.' The same term is also used for a cash dispenser, almost as if every now and again you might get more money from it than you expect: 'Ah wis gauny pay ye back the noo but Ah couldny find a puggy that wis workin.'

To take a puggy is to become extremely angry: 'Keep the heid! We'll never get it sorted if ye take a puggy at it lik that.'

Someone who is highly inebriated or who has eaten too much may be described as **full as a puggy**. Similarly, if a person makes a habit of such overindulgence he may end up as **fat as a puggy**.

Puggy work means hard physical labour, the same as donkey work: 'It's aw right fur you sittin on yer arse giein oot yer orders, an it's me that's tae dae the puggy work.'

pulley A frame of wooden rods on which clothes can be dried indoors, lowered and hoisted to a kitchen ceiling by an arrangement of ropes: 'Is ma new shirt on that pulley?'

pump This is used onomatopoeically to mean *fart*: 'Who pumped?' 'Was that a wee pump Ah heard?'

It can also mean to have sexual intercourse: 'He has pumped me an bolted.'

pun A pound in weight: 'Run doon tae the fruit shoap an get us a pun a carrots an three pun a totties, there's a good wee soul.'

The phrase **ther's no two pun a her hingin the right way** is a graphic way of saying that someone is rather oddly shaped.

punny *or* **punny eccy** School slang, used by both staff and pupils, for a punishment exercise, i.e. a written piece of work given to a child as punishment for some classroom crime: 'Ah canny come oot till Ah've finished this punny eccy fur Aul Kipper.'

punt-up *or* **puntie-up** To give someone one of these is to help him get over a wall or on top of some obstacle by standing with your back to it and making a kind of stirrup with your interlaced fingers for the climber to put a foot into: 'You gie me a puntie-up an Ah'll pull ye up efter me.'

pure Used as an adjective or adverb, this has got nothing to do with being pristine but means total, totally, absolute, absolutely: 'She went pure mental when she heard.' 'That's a pure brilliant idea!' 'You are pure sad, pal.'

Comin doon the Queenie? The model boats are on the pond. The day...

Queenie, the A familiar name for the Queens Park, a large public park on the South Side: 'Comin doon the Queenie? The model boats are on the pond the day.'

queer In the phrase **a queer difference** the word means great, not strange: 'There's a queer difference between your top line and what you come away with in your hand.'

queerie Any odd or eccentric individual: 'Ah've always thought her man was a bit of a queerie.'

queued out A term used to describe any place or event that is very busy or crowded: 'We tried tae get inty the Odeon tae see that *Braveheart II*, but when we seen how queued oot it wis we just came away.'

quoted This term comes from the world of betting and refers to the odds quoted by the bookies for certain racehorses or other competitors. In everyday speech **well-quoted** means highly-thought-of or respected: 'Ah hear that councillor you've got's well-quoted.'

The opposite of this is **not quoted**, i.e. not reckoned as being up to much: 'As for you, you're no quoted in this business, so shut yer yap.'

Rab Haw, the Glesga Glutton...

ra In broad Glaswegian the word *the* often comes out as **ra**: 'Ra boays played pure mince.'

Rab Ha' *or* **Haw** A name applied to any glutton or even to someone who merely has a big appetite: 'Ah went tae get merr soup but Rab Ha' here had snaffled the lot.'

Rab Ha', or Robert Hall, was a real person, a vagrant who died in 1843 having become famous throughout the west of Scotland for his unparallelled eating capacity. His rapacious appetite was often the subject of wagers and it seems that the smart money was always on Rab. The story is told of one such occasion when Rab was tasked with consuming a whole calf (except for the skin). The unfortunate beast was served up to Rab in the form of pies, which he duly despatched. Rab was then heard to ask where was this calf he was meant to be eating.

As well as being used in the name for more than one Glasgow restaurant, Rab is commemorated in the following rhyme:

Rab Ha' the Glesga Glutton
et ten loaves an a leg a mutton.

rag Someone who loses his temper is said to **lose the rag**: 'The boay said it wis an accident ... there nae need tae lose the rag.'

raging Extremely angry: 'Ah knew she'd be ragin so Ah didny bother phonin.'

rammy A **rammy** is a violent disturbance or any busy or bustling crowd: 'That wis some rammy when they said the tickets were sold out.'
   The word is also used as a slang term for a glass bottle that has a deposit on it: 'He's away tae the shoap wi a bag full a rammies.'
   To rammy is to take part in a violent disturbance: 'There's too much rammyin at the fitba these days ... an that's just the players.'

randan Someone who is **on the randan** is on a spree of wild behaviour, usually involving debauchery and drunkenness: 'Is that your second sherry ye're on? It's well seen ye're on the randan tonight.'

rare Used to describe anything excellent: 'Ye make a rare cup a tea, hen!' 'Ye want tae have seen that fillum ... it wis rerr!'

rat In a similar way to **ra** (meaning *the*), **rat** is a broad Glaswegian form of *that*: 'Did ye see rat? Rat's terrible, so it is.'

rattle To **rattle** a part of a person's body is to hit him there: 'Ah'll rattle yer ear if Ah get ye!' **To rattle** a place is to burgle or rob it: 'Ah hear yer hoose got rattled the other night.'
   To rattle around is to be up and about, present and lively: 'Ah thought she'd have the weans down by now but they're still rattlin around.'

rebel song A song that celebrates the deeds of the Irish Republicans: 'Ah don't think they make karaoke tapes wi rebel songs on them.'

red *or* **rid Red raw** is a description applied to parts of one's person that, through being very cold or wet, are sore and reddened: 'The weans' hauns were rid raw when they came in from makin their snowman.'

Red rotten means very bad, absolute rubbish: 'That play he took us tae was red rotten. There was nae story tae it.'

red biddy See under **biddy**.

refreshment A **wee refreshment** is a euphemism for an alcoholic drink: 'We'll maybe partake of a wee refreshment on the way through to Edinburgh.' This has given rise to various jokey ways of referring to drunkenness, such as **well-refreshed** or **over-refreshed**: 'The club has received complaints that over-refreshed patrons are making too much noise when leaving the premises.'

remmy Short for 'remedial', as in a remedial teacher who specialises in helping those with learning difficulties. This came to be used, cruelly, as an insult for somebody considered stupid or slow: 'It's no exactly rocket science, ya remmy!"

rhyme off To recite a list, usually to the boredom of the listeners: 'Ah'm sick a hearin the wee tube rhymin aff aw the burds he's podgered.'

Riddrie Hilton A nickname for H.M. Prison Barlinnie, located in the Riddrie area on the north-east side of Glasgow.

riddy A **riddy** is a red (or **rid**) face indicative of high embarrassment. It can also mean the cause of the embarrassment: 'That wis a pure riddy when Ah drapped that plate.' To **take a riddy** is to blush: 'She took a big riddy when he walked in.'

riggin Rigging; a football slang term for the goal-net: 'He took wan look up an bang! it's in the riggin.'

right If a person wants to cast doubt on the likelihood or truth of something someone else has said he might say **that'll** (or **that will**) **be right**: 'What, work longer hours for the same money? Aye, that'll be right!' Unusually, this expression has its own piece of rhyming slang: **that'll be shining bright**, occasionally shortened to **that'll be shining**.

Right is also used to mean ready, all set: 'Are ye right? Come on then.'

rings Someone who is being violently sick is often said to be **vomiting rings round** himself. I suppose the idea is that the unfortunately afflicted individual is able to direct the flow away from his own person but is otherwise helpless: 'Ah don't know what he's been eatin, but he's been vomitin rings roon hissel aw mornin, the soul.'

rip Used in particular to mean to cut or slash someone with a blade: 'Ah'll rip ye wide, ya wee crapbag.'

ripped A slang word meaning under the influence of alcohol or illicit drugs. More elaborate versions include **ripped out yer nut** and **ripped out yer tits**.

road To be or get **in your own road** is to be very clumsy in performing some activity: 'Ah don't know what's up wi me the day. Ah'm just getting in ma own road.'

When the phrase **on the road out** is applied to a person, this is a euphemistic way to say that they are dying: 'Ah doubt that's yer granmaw on the road out this time.'

rocket A crazy or volatile person, presumably from the idea of the firework shooting off noisily and wildly into the sky: 'Whit's that mad wee rocket shoutin the odds aboot?'

roll about To laugh uproariously: 'Get um tae tell ye aboot when he got lost in Embra. We were aw rollin aboot when he telt us.'

rollie A hand-rolled cigarette: 'Look at the size a the rollie he's giein us! Ye'd need a poultice tae get a draw oot it!'

rooked Completely out of money, skint: 'We reckoned we'd taken enough dosh for the whole weekend but on Saturday mornin that was us rooked.'

room and kitchen A tenement flat, small, but a cut above a *single end* in that it has two rooms as well as a bathroom. One of the rooms has a cooker and sink, and some occupants will

use this room as a sitting room and keep the other as a bedroom only. Other people are happy to sleep in the kitchen's
bed-recess and use the other room as a sitting room.

Rossy A Glasgow pronunciation of Rothesay, Isle of Bute,
traditionally popular as a holiday resort for citizens: 'Ma
mammy says we're gaun tae Rossy on the Waverley!'

rotten drunk Extremely drunk: 'Ah came in the door an
nearly fell ower the big waster lyin there rotten drunk.' This is
sometimes shortened to **rotten**: 'No way is she gaun anywhere.
She's pure rotten.'

Roukie, the A familiar name for Rouken Glen, an extensive
public park on the South Side: 'Does the thirty-eight bus take
ye the length a the Roukie?'

Royal, the A common abbreviation for the Royal Infirmary:
'She was a Sister in the Royal before she came to Yorkhill.'

rubber ear To **throw** or **sling someone a rubber ear** means to
deliberately fail to hear someone, to ignore him pointedly, or
to turn down someone who asks you out: 'Ah tried oot the
patter on this wee doll but she slung us a rubber ear.'
  Also used as a verb: '"No hard feelins," he says, the snidey
wee get. Ah just rubber-eared um.'

rubber man To **do a** or **one's rubber man** is to be so drunk that
you cannot stand upright without swaying around, holding
onto something, or looking as if your legs might buckle: 'Ah
seen yer wee brother daein his rubber man in George Square
last night.'

Rubber Yacht, the A nickname, used mainly by taxi-drivers,
for the Rubaiyyat pub, a well-known West-End landmark in
Byres Road.

Ruglonian A native of Rutherglen, which is often pronounced
'Ruglen': 'Don't cry me a Glaswegian, sonny boy. Ah'm a
Ruglonian, born an bred.'

rummle A **rummle in the sheets** is a less than romantic way to

140

describe a sexual encounter: 'Know what the cheeky peasant says tae me? "Fancy a rummle in the sheets, doll?" Ah took ma haun aff his jaw!'

rumped An extremely short haircut is often said to have been **rumped right inty the wid**. See **wid²**.

run To **run about daft** is to be very busy, under pressure, especially if this involves going to and from several places: 'That wean's got me runnin aboot daft tryin tae get the right batteries for that game a his.'

Another version of this is **run aboot stupit**.

runnie Used especially by schoolchildren, to **take a runnie at** something is to take a few paces back and then run towards it: 'Ah bet Ah could jump that waw if Ah took a runnie at it.'

run-out Someone who **does a run-out** is guilty of consuming a meal in a restaurant, asking for the bill, then leaving swifly without paying while the waiter fetches the bill: 'Hear aboot the Irish run-oot? They ordered a meal an ran oot withoot eatin it!'

. blaw the simmit aff ye .

sad Apart from its usual meanings, this word is used, especially by schoolkids, to label anything unpleasant or unfair: 'When I tell you to do something, child, I'm afraid that "That's pure sad, Miss," is not an appropriate response.'

A **sad case** or **saddie** is a slang term for someone considered crazy, especially in a dangerous way: 'Did ye hear what that big sad case done?'

Saltmarket The phrase **all the comforts of the Saltmarket** is a piece of irony meaning no comforts at all, no mod cons: 'Aw we're needin is a bit a carpet doon, the watter on, somethin tae sit on, an we'll have aw the comforts of the Saltmarket!'

sangwidge An odd version of *sandwich*: 'The French fancies do look nice, but I think I'll just have a wee cheese sangwidge.'

sanny This can mean a sandshoe: 'Don't forget yer sannies for gym tomorrow.' It can also be a sandwich: 'Ah've et nothin aw day but a packet a sannies oot the garage.'

Sarry Heid The nickname of the Saracen's Head public

142

house in the Gallowgate, reputedly the oldest pub in the city, although the original building no longer stands. This pub is proverbial for hard drinking and boisterousness: 'We'll nick inty the Sarry Heid for a couple a pints a shammy before we go inty the concert.'

Scabby Aggie An abusive name, particularly among schoolchildren, for any female considered to be unclean: 'Don't tell us ye've tae sit next tae *that* Scabby Aggie?'

scabby touch Used in a children's game like tig. The difference is that it can begin spontaneously, as when someone is adjudged to have come in contact with something disgusting. He is then told he has the scabby touch and is obliged to touch someone else in order to pass on, and free himself of, the vile contagion: 'When Ah telt um Ah wis efter a refund he looked at us like Ah'd gied um the scabby touch.'

scadge A slang term for a tramp or disreputable-looking person: 'Gauny no staun next tae us, ya scadge? Ye'll gie us a showin up.' The word sounds as if it might be connected with *scavenger*.

The description **scadgey** comes from this and can be applied to anything considered dirty, unpleasant or in any way contemptible: 'Ye're no comin oot wi me in that scadgey wee top.' 'The second flat we looked at wis kinna scadgey.'

scheme A housing estate, especially any of the postwar council estates in such areas as Drumchapel or Darnley. Although great strides have been taken in improving these places they still tend to be tarred with the brush of isolation, deprivation and lack of amenities: 'There's no a street in the scheme that disny have boarded-up windies.'

schemie (pronounced *skeemy*) A rather disparaging term for a person, especially a youth, who lives in a scheme: 'That pub's full of schemies on a Friday night.'

A variation of this is **schemebo**.

scooby If you **don't have a scooby** you don't have a clue, have no idea at all about the subject in question: 'Ah asked him if he knew how tae work it, but he disny have a scooby'. This comes from the rhyming slang for *clue*, **scooby doo**, inspired by the eponymous canine hero of an American children's cartoon series seen on TV in this country from the early 1970s onwards.

scoof A slang word meaning to steal, or take charge of something that seems to lack an obvious owner: 'When Ah came back fae the lavvy some ratbag had scoofed the placky bag Ah left under ma seat.'

To **scoof** an empty house is to break into it and strip out everything of possible value, such as radiators, pipes, cables, etc: 'There flats wi the boarded-up windies have aw been scoofed long since.

scrappie A scrap-metal dealer or his yard: 'Ah've seen motors in better nick than that lyin in the scrappie.'

scratcher A bed, obviously with the suggestion that it is inhabited by fleas as well as the nominal occupant: 'Ye'll be waitin long enough if ye're waitin fur that durty aul rascal tae get oot his scratcher.'

screw If you want someone to calm down or start behaving more sensibly you might tell him to **screw the bobbin** or **screw the nut**: 'The gaffer's just lookin for an excuse tae get a few bodies oot the door, so ye better screw the nut here.'

screwtap A screwtop bottle, usually, but not exclusively, for beer: 'Gie um a couple a Guinness screwtaps an a chair oot the back an he'll be happy as Larry.' 'Whit's up? Screwtap wine no good enough fur ye?'

The most famous use of the term has to be in Matt McGinn's version of *Raindrops Keep Falling on my Head*, the Bacharach-David song: *Screwtaps are Fallin on ma Heid.*

scud[1] Someone who is **in the scud** or **in the scuddy** is in the nude: 'The durty beasts were takin photies of each other in the scud!' **In the bare scud** means the same thing but suggests that the speaker is even more shocked. **Scuddy**

is also sometimes used as an adjective: 'We went tae this beach an there were aw these scuddy punters stoatin aboot!'

A **scuddy-book** is a pornographic magazine: 'Ah wis cleanin under his bed an fun a pile a scuddy-books, the durty wee devil!'

scud² A slang term for wine: 'See's a bottle a Beck's an a glass a red scud.'

see Used to introduce the subject of remarks that immediately follow: 'See that wummin doon the stair? She says she knows your Isa.' This is a useful device for people who like to break in a subject gradually rather than breenge straight to the point: 'See that guy wi the baseball hat? See his dug? See where he lets it dae its business? Shouldny be allowed!'

See if is used to introduce a question seeking information: 'See if Ah ask your pal for a len a his lawnmower, would he gie us it?' This can also be another way of saying *if*: 'See if Ah've tae tell you again, Ah'll tan yer erse.'

A strange local construction, seeming to imply an uncanny ability to observe oneself in a detached way, is **Ah've seen me**, meaning 'there have been times when I have been . . .': 'Ah'm hopeless at buyin claes. Ah've seen me spendin the hale day up the toon an comin hame wi hee-haw.'

session A period spent drinking alcohol is often called a **session** or **bevvy session**: 'Ah used tae go for a lunchtime pint wi them till it startit turnin inty a session every time.' Some people shorten this to **sesh**: 'Know what Ah fancy? A right good-goin sesh wi ma mates.'

shady Used to describe anything undesirable: 'Have we tae dae aw this fur the morra? That's pure shady, Miss!'

shape A disparaging term for anyone considered physically odd-looking: 'Did ye see that wee shape she ended up dancin wi?'

Shaws, the A familiar name for the Pollokshaws area, on the South Side: 'Oh him? He's wan a the queer folk a the Shaws.'

sheet To **put a sheet round** in a place of work is to make a collection of money for someone who is leaving, getting married, having a baby, and so on: 'Did ye hear? Aul Miseryguts isny lettin us put a sheet roon for wee Sheila.'

The cash so collected is known as **sheet money**: 'That sheet money came in awful handy for baby clothes.'

To **put to** someone's **sheet** is to make your contribution: 'Right, emdy that hasny pit tae this sheet, get yer money in noo.'

The expression probably originated in the collection of cash or goods in an actual bedsheet carried round in a neighbourhood.

sheuch *or* **shuch** (pronounced like *shuck*, but with the *ch* as in *loch*) A Scots word for *ditch*, used locally to mean the cleft of the buttocks: 'He gave um a toe-ender, right in the sheuch!'

The phrase **up the sheuch** means in a state of error, barking up the wrong tree: 'If that's what ye think ye're up the sheuch, mate.'

Shields, the A familiar name for the Pollkshields area on the South Side: 'Is the Shields no a dry area?' 'If it is, Ah know the guy that drank it dry!'

shilling This pre-decimal coin lives on in the phrases **not the full shilling** and **threepence off the shilling**, which both mean 'not right in the head', not possessed of a fully functioning brain.

shirrackin Someone who gets a **shirrackin** is being given a row, or being made the target of verbal abuse: 'Her maw gied her a right shirrackin for no comin in last night.' 'Ye should a heard the shirrackin the driver got when he got back onty the bus.'

shite-awful Of extremely low quality: 'Efter aw that big build-up it wis a shite-awful gemme.'

shiters To **put the shiters up** a person is to terrify him: 'Tell him ye're gauny shop him, just tae put the shiters up the wee nyaff.'

shoodery One step up from a coal-carry, that is, the person carried is positioned on the carrier's **shooders** (shoulders), with a leg on each side of the carrier's neck: 'Her boyfriend was givin her a shoodery so's she could see the stage, an the big eejit went an drapt her.'

Shooey *or* **Shoo**; **Shuggy** *or* **Shug** Local nicknames for anyone called *Hugh*. For some unexplained reason Glaswegians often insert a phantom *s* in pronouncing certain words beginning with *h*. The name *Hugh* is one of these: 'Her man wis Sir Shoo Fraser's chauffeur.' The same applies to the surname *Hughes*: 'Is that the John Shooz that usety play fur Celtic?' It's anybody's guess as to how Hugh turns into **Shuggy** or **Shug**.

shoot To shoot means to leave, especially quickly: 'Ah'll need tae shoot in a couple a minutes.' It may be that this is shortened from the phrase **shoot the crow**, meaning the same thing: 'He'd shot the crow by the time we got back.' I don't know why firing at a bird should be equated with departure; some say it is rhyming slang, i.e. *shoot the crow* for *go*, but this doesn't work when, as often happens, people say **shoot the** *craw*.

shot Used in slang to mean any item or individual. For example, a Highlandman might be referred to as 'an Angus Og shot', and a homosexual as 'a bent shot': 'Do you want the fifty-pence or one pound size?' 'Gie's the ten-bob shot.'

This probably comes from betting parlance, in which, say, a horse starting at odds of 10-1 would be a 'ten-to-one shot'.

shots each A local expression meaning turn and turn about: 'There's only wan joystick between yeez, so it's tae be shots each, right?'

shout To shout someone is to call him, alert him to something, such as the fact that it's time for him to get up: 'Ma Da shouts us at hauf-six.' 'Shout us when we get to Thornwood Drive, will you please, driver?'

To shout on a person is to call out his name to attract his attention: 'There sumdy shoutin on you roun the back.'

147

shows, the A funfair or carnival: 'We all went to the shows at Bellahouston Park.'

shuffle An old-fashioned term for a betting shop: 'See if ye're passin the shuffle, gauny stick this line oan fur us?'

shuge A Glaswegian variant of *huge*, undergoing the same change in pronunciation as *Hugh* to *Shoo*: 'Sumdy's dug a big shuge hole in the road.'

shunk *or* **shunkie** Slang words for a toilet: 'Ma eyeballs are floatin. Mind ma pint till Ah dive tae the shunk.'
   This probably comes from the famous local manufacturer of sanitary ware, Shanks of Barrhead, whose name would be prominently displayed on the equipment.

shunt **To shunt** someone is to reject or dismiss them, especially when they are keen to establish a romantic relationship with you: 'They tried tae buy us a drink, but we took wan look at the shoes they hud oan and shunted them.'

shy **A shy** is a throw-in in a game of football: 'The big donkey's last shot was that far off the mark it went out for a shy on the other side.' **To shy** the ball is to use it in a throw-in: 'He shied it right inty the goalmouth.'

sick Someone who takes time off work because of illness is said to be **on the sick.**
   To **sicken someone's happiness** is to spoil their fun, make their life a misery: 'Would it no sicken yer happiness havin tae go hame tae a greetin face like that?' **A sickener** is something bad that happens to a person, something that is a huge disappointment: 'The very next week after she changed her lottery numbers they came up. What a sickener!'
   If someone believes that they have won an argument they might crow over their opponent by saying to them: **sickened you!**

sideyways This can mean sideways: 'It'll no go that way; we'll need to try it sideyways.' It is also a jocular version of suicide:

'If that car alarm doesny stoap soon Ah'm gauny commit sideyways!'

signwriter A slang term for an unemployed person, i.e. someone who signs on, is a **signwriter for the Social Security**.

sillywatter Like **cheekywatter**, a name for alcoholic drink that includes an indication of how it is conceived as affecting the consumer: 'Whit? Have you been on the sillywatter? Gie's a break!'

sin Anything that is regarded as unjust or pitiable may be described as **a sin**: 'The wee soul had tae walk hame in aw that snaw. A sin, so it was.'

sine-died A slang term meaning permanently barred: 'He's sayin there's nae way you're getting back in there. Ye're sine-died, he says.' This comes from the football practice (never very common, it seems) of banning for life a player who has committed some unforgiveable offence (*sine die* being Latin, literally 'without a day'.

singin Like *laughing* this is often used to mean very happy or lucky: 'If this weather keeps up till the weekend we're singin.'

singin ginger See **ginger**.

single (often pronounced *sing*-ull) On a chip-shop menu, anything with the word **single** in front of it is sold on its own, without chips: 'Gie's a haggis supper, two pokes a chips an a single fish.'

A **single** is a loose cigarette, sold individually in some shops to those not in funds: 'Here Ah'm gaspin fur a drag an Ah huvny the price ae a tipped single.'

single end A local term for a one-room tenement flat: 'Ah wis dragged up in a single end in Maryhill an look at us noo.'

sink To **sink the boot on** someone is to kick him: 'The dirty big animal sunk the boot on the goalie when he was on the deck.'

In football, **to sink** a player is to bring him down with a hard tackle: 'Sumdy sink that wee striker for goodness sake!'

sinker A descriptive term for a dirty look or the kind of glance that makes the receiver feel like crawling away to hide: 'The guy wouldny shut up till wee Elspeth drew him a right sinker.'

sittie-doon *or* **sittie-in** When describing a meal, these mean the opposite of **carry-out**: 'It's no often Ah get taken oot fur a sittie-doon dinner.'

skate If you win something easily you might be said to **skate** it: 'The Jags'll skate that gemme the morra.'

skelf A **skelf** can be a sliver of wood that gets stuck under the skin, especially, but not exclusively, of a finger or toe: 'Ah telt ye ye would get skelfs in yer bum if ye sat on that fence.' It can also mean a very skinny or undersized person: 'Imagine Big Gus bein married tae a wee skelf like her.'

skelly A description applied to any person whose eyes cross or who has a squint: 'Look at yer aul granny gaun skelly tryin tae thread that needle.'

skelp This Scots word for smack is also used locally in the phrase **skelp it**, meaning to work briskly at a job: 'We'll need tae skelp it tae get this finished by dinnertime.'

   On the skelp means on a wild night out or drinking spree: 'Some state he's in. Looks like he's been on the skelp for a week.'

skinto A local variation of *skint*, i.e. out of money: 'Okay, wan merr can a ginger each an that's yer whack, or ye'll have yer aul granda skinto.'

skip Someone who **skips** something, especially paying for something, gets away with avoiding it: 'They school weans aw pile on the bus at the wan time an the hauf a them skip their fares.'

skitter A **skitter** can mean a small amount of something: 'There only a wee skitter a milk left in the jug.'

skittery Used to describe anything small or contemptible:

'Ah'm still starvin after that skittery wee helpin ye gave us.'

It is also applied to food or drink that it is feared will cause diarrhoea: 'They curries're too skittery for me.'

skitterywinter Traditionally, a name applied to the last person to turn up for work in a factory, shipyard, office, etc on Hogmanay (in some workplaces, also on Fair Friday). The unfortunate latecomer would be greeted by his workmates banging loudly on any suitable surface. The term is still heard in wider use to mean anyone who is dilatory or lags behind: 'How is it you're always the last out yer pit, skitterywinter?'

skoosh Any fizzy soft drink: 'Ah could murder a big boatle a skoosh!'

A **skoosh** or **skoosh-case** is something that is accomplished with no great effort: 'Ah tried tae convince aul greetin-face that the flittin would be a skoosh-case but ye can tell her nothin.'

To **skoosh** something or **skoosh it** is to accomplish it with ease: 'Just concentrate on yer three-point turns an ye'll skoosh that drivin test.'

Skooshed is another word for drunk: 'He wis that skooshed ye couldny make oot a word he wis sayin.'

slabberchops A name to call someone, especially a baby, who dribbles or salivates: 'Put a bib on wee Slabberchops or that Babygro'll be soakin in five minutes.'

slag To insult or make uncomplimentary remarks about a person it **to slag** him: 'Never mind them slaggin ye . . . they're pig-ignorant, the lot a them.' A **slag** is an insulting remark.

Schoolkids and other youths delight in slagging each other continually, to the extent of handing out derogatory nicknames known as **slag-names.** Most will cheerfully tell you what their slag-name is.

slaughtered A slang term for drunk: 'Tae hell wi this caper! Ah'm away oot tae get slaughtered.'

sluch To eat or drink something, for example soup, making noises with one's mouth: 'He gies ye a right showin up wi his sluchin.'

slug **To slug** a liquid is to drink it straight from the bottle: 'Could you no use a glass instead a sluggin it oot the boatle?'

A slug is a drink from a bottle: 'Gies a slug a that skoosh afore ye finish it.'

slush A nickname for tea: 'Wait an Ah'll stick the kettle on for a wee cup a slush.'

smell To make something, especially the breath, smell of something: 'Eatin that garlicky food really smells yer breath.'

snakie Short for snakebite, the drink concocted of cider and lager: 'If she's been on the snakies aw night it's nae wunner she's honkin her load.'

snibbed Teenagers all over the English-speaking world know what it is to be 'grounded', i.e. confined to your home and not allowed out to enjoy yourself, but in Glasgow you are not grounded but **snibbed**. This comes from the snib used to lock a door.

snidey Counterfeit or fake in some way. A **snidey cheque** is one that is sure to bounce.

snotter Someone who has a cold or a runny nose may have it said of him that **the snotters are blindin** (or **trippin**) him.

snottery Used as a general term of disapproval or contempt: 'Is that snottery wee drap aw the tea that's left?' 'What's that snottery aul get lookin at us fur?'

snotterybeak A name to call someone with a runny nose: 'Will sumdy gie Snotterybeak the len ae a hankie? That sniffin's drivin me up the waw!'

snyster A term used to mean a little bite of anything tasty, especially something sweet: 'Ah could just go a wee snyster afore ma tea.'

so A common local usage is the instant confirmation of something you have just said (a double positive?) by means of phrases beginning with *so*: 'Ah'm getting right fed up wi this, so Ah am.' 'That hat suits ye, so it does.'

So I will is an ironic phrase that seems to express agreement but actually means the opposite: 'You've to have this finished by tomorrow.' 'Aye, an so Ah wull.'

soapdogger An insult, implying a lack of personal hygiene brought about by avoiding soap. See **dog**. Some people say **soapdodger**.

Society man, the Not someone who moves in refined circles, but a local term for a representative of the Co-operative Insurance Society who calls at people's homes to collect periodical policy payments: 'Is this no the night for the Society man?'

sodie Soda. 'Ah could just go a wee sodie scone.' 'Ye get a rare loaf a sodie breid oot that bakers.' 'See's a Remy an sodie watter, barman.'

Sons of William A collective term for Protestants (especially Rangers supporters), deriving, of course, from their hero William of Orange: 'Bemused citizens looked on as an advance party of the Sons of William took over one of the city-centre bars in anticipation of tomorrow night's UEFA Cup game.'

sook To call a person **a sook** is to accuse him of being a toady, trying to ingratiate himself with somebody else, especially his superiors: 'Ah bet you've finished yer homework already, ya wee sook.'

To sook in is to try to ingratiate yourself with someone: 'There would be merr work done aroon here if you put in a full shift instead a spendin hauf yer time sookin in wi the gaffer.'

sookie sweeties are hard sweets, such as boilings, that have to be sucked rather than chewed: 'Mind an get yer Grannie sookie sweeties ... she canny go the caramels wi they new wallies.'

Sooside, the The area of Glasgow south of the river Clyde: 'Ma Maw'll no move away fae the Sooside.' An inhabitant of this area is called a **Soosider**.

sore hand A large jam sandwich. The joke is in comparing the white bread and red jam with a bloodstained bandage.

sore wan A painful blow or injury: 'The wean got a right sore wan runnin inty that glass door.'

soul (sometimes pronounced to rhyme with *howl*) This is used to express pity or affection for someone: 'She's that happy wi her new dolly, the wee soul!' 'Could somebody no gie that poor aul soul a haun across the road?'

sovvy ring A bulky gold ring incorporating a sovereign coin: 'He got his haun stuck in the video wi they daft sovvy rings a his.'

Spam Valley A disparaging term for any suburban area of good housing and amenities, in which live many people, especially younger couples, who have trouble affording it. Such people are said to have to economise to the extent of being obliged to include lots of Spam in their diet: 'It's a cheap and cheerful café-bar popular with the local Spam Valley set.'

spare A general term for unattached members of the opposite sex: 'There's always plenty of spare at Big Mandy's parties.'

special A term used by many brewers for their heavy beers: 'They've only got special or lager on draught.' **Spesh** is a shortened form of this: 'Two pints a spesh when ye're ready, Tony.'

specky A term applied to any spectacle-wearing person: 'Hey Specky! See's ower the mulk.' 'Ah thought her man would be nice-lookin, no a specky wee nyaff.'

Spiders, the A nickname for Queen's Park F.C., deriving from the fact that the black-and-white hoops on their jerseys are reminiscent of a spider's web. Although not in the top flight of Glasgow clubs, Queen's Park have a long history and loyal fan-base, and their home ground, Hampden Park, is also the national stadium and home of the Scottish Football Museum.

spinbin A slang term for a psychiatric hospital: 'Are ye still workin in the spinbin?'

spittin feathers A slang term meaning dry-mouthed, extremely thirsty: 'Brilliant, eh? Ye come in from half a shift in the garden, spittin feathers, an some lazy bassa's swallied aw the lagers.'

spur To **take the spur** is to become annoyed, take offence: 'Aw c'mon, Ah'm only kiddin ye. Nae need tae take the spur.'

squaddie A schoolteachers' term for a P.E. teacher. Perhaps this originated in the fact that many of these were traditionally ex-servicemen.

square go See under **go**.

square sausage Another name for Lorne sausage, sausage meat formed into a rough oblong and then cut into slices: 'Ma aunty in Canada says there's a shop in Toronto that sells squerr sausage an Irn Bru.' Café diners who are strangers to Glasgow are often surprised to find they are eating this instead of a link when they order a roll and sausage.

squinty A local version of *squint*, meaning crooked or askew: 'Only a bum joiner would leave the thing lookin as squinty as that.'

stairhead (often pronounced *sterrheid*) In tenement closes this is the name given to the landing at the top of each flight of stairs. A **stairhead toilet** was a communal lavatory on such a landing in the days before inside facilities became the norm. As you might expect, a **stairhead window** is a window at a stairhead: 'It's freezin oot in the close wi that sterrheid windy open.'

stakes Another term borrowed from the world of gambling, in this case from the titles of horse races, such as the *Queen Elizabeth II Stakes*. In local slang this is used to give a descriptive name to any situation: 'If Ah canny get ma hauns oan some readies afore the end a the month it'll be pure desperation stakes.'

stank A street drain, or the metal grille that covers it: 'Ah drapt a pound coin an it rolled doon that stank.' The phrase **doon the stank** is used in the same way as the English *down the drain*: 'It's just money doon the stank tryin tae keep that place gaun.'

stank-dodger A slang term for a skinny person, implying that such individuals have to avoid street drains for fear of falling down one: 'What's stank-dodger like you need tae be on a diet for?'

stank monster In local slang, a person so ugly or repulsive that they might just have crawled out of a stank: 'Nice-lookin? That's a total stank monster, man!'

stauner An erection of the penis, from *staun*, the Scots for *stand*.

steakie A steak-knife: 'The mad bastart went fur us wi a steakie!'

steam There are several Glasgow expressions connected with this word, perhaps reflecting the city's historical involvement in the construction of ships and railway engines.

To **get steamed in** to a thing or person is to set about it or him with great vigour: 'If we get steamed inty this paper-strippin we'll manage a pint before they shut.' 'The boy took a pure maddy an got steamed inty the pair a them.'

Somebody who has **a good head of steam about him** is obviously elevated by drink, like a steam engine stoked up and ready to chug along: 'Ye had a good head a steam aboot ye when Ah bumped inty ye that night.'

A **steamer** is a slang term for a drinking bout: 'When wis the last time you *wereny* on a steamer on a Friday night?'

Someone who is drunk may be described as **steamin** or **steamin drunk**: 'If comin hame steamin drunk every night is his plan he'll be oot that door.' **Steamed** or **steamed up** are similarly used: 'They get steamed up on the cheap wine an go lookin for bother.'

steamboats Another word for drunk: 'Ah've seen the guy totally steamboats in the middle of the day.' Some say that the origin of this picturesque expression lies in the traditional Glasgow pastime of going for pleasure cruises down the Firth of Clyde. Apparently, men would give the excuse of 'going to take a look at the engines' to pay a visit to the bar. It then became proverbial that people alighting from such steamboats would seem to have difficulty in regaining their land legs.

steamie A local term for a public laundry, formerly common all over the city but now mostly a thing of the past. As Tony Roper's popular play *The Steamie* showed to perfection, these places were often the hub of their community and were renowned as hotbeds of gossip, and it is this aspect of their existence that lives on in the phrase **the talk of the steamie**, applied to anything or anyone considered scandalous: 'The state she was in at the awards ceremony is the current talk of the steamie in media circles.'

steelies A slang term for steel-toecapped protective working boots: 'Ah'd like tae get inty that toerag's heid wi ma steelies.'

stenked Yet another word for drunk. A philologist might have a field day investigating why so many of these terms begin with *st-*.

stick When a person loses patience with someone else who is sulking or in a huff, he may say to them: 'Stick, bubbly!' meaning, roughly, 'Have it your own way, crybaby. I don't care any more.'

stiffen To batter a person, especially to knock him unconscious: 'Ah'll stiffen the both a yeez if ye don't cut oot aw this argy-bargyin.' I suppose the idea is really that the attacked person will be killed and thus undergo rigor mortis.

stinkin rotten Literally, rotted to the point of becoming smelly, this is used to describe anything considered very bad: 'She telt us that wis a good story, an here it wis wan a the most stinkin rotten books Ah ever opened.'

stir Someone who deliberately causes trouble between others is said to **stir it**: 'Never mind what that wee cow says. She's just tryin tae stir it.' Someone who behaves in this manner may be called a **stirrer**. When someone wants to tell another person that a third party in their company is stirring it, this can be done silently by miming the motions of stirring a pot.

stoat This is the local pronunciation of the Scots *stot*, meaning bounce: 'Gauny no stoat yer baw ootside this windy? Yer Da's goat a sair heid.' In betting circles the word is used to mean win, as in: 'If this line stoats Ah'll get ye a doner kebab.'

Stoat doon is what particularly heavy rain is said to do: 'It wisny takin the time tae rain . . . it wis stoatin doon.'

To stoat aboot is to circulate, move around in a not particularly purposeful manner: 'Her and her mammy like tae stoat aboot the shops on a Thursday evenin.'

A stoat-up is the term used in football for the practice of restarting play with a dropped ball.

Anything excellent, but especially an attractive member of the opposite sex, may be called a **stoater**: 'He hit him a stoater right in the coupon.' 'That wis a big stoater ye nipped last night.'

Stoatin is used to mean two things: one is very good, as in 'That wis a stoatin dinner we hud roon at your place.' The other is stale, applied to food that has gone too hard to eat and would therefore be liable to bounce if dropped: 'If they scones are stoatin just pap them in the bin.'

A stoat-the-baw is a slang term for paedophile, from the comparison, perhaps, of patting a child's head to bouncing a ball. **A stoatybumper** is another slang term for anything excellent, being an amalgam of two other such words, *stoater* and *bumper*. 'Is this for me? Aw, ye're a wee stoatybumper, so ye are!'

stooky This Scots word for plaster, derived from *stucco*, is used in various local expressions. **A stooky** is a plaster cast on a broken limb: 'Can Ah write ma name on yer stooky?' It is also used to mean a stupid or spiritless person, comparing them to a statue: 'Are you just gauny staun there lik a stooky?'

To stooky a person (like **stiffen**) is to hit him extremely hard, especially to knock him out: 'What did ye have tae go an stooky the guy for?'

stooshie An uproar or row: 'He's a popular guy, and there'll be some stooshie if ye sack him.'

storm damage A local version of 'a few slates missing', i.e. an implication that someone is not right in the head: 'Ah wouldny pay too much attention tae what he tells ye. There's a fair bit a storm damage there.'

Also used in adjectival form: 'C'moan oot a here. This guy's storm-damaged.'

stormer A slang term for anything considered outstandingly good: 'Mackay made sure of the points with an absolute stormer of a goal in the eighty-ninth minute.'

stotious (pronounced *stoe-shuss*) This is another word, probably an import from Ireland in this case, for drunk: 'Get him up tae his bed; he's stotious.'

stove To **stove in** or **get stoved in** means to partake of something enthusiastically: 'Help yersels tae champagne, lads, an get stoved inty they canapés.'

stowed (often pronounced to rhyme with *loud*) or **stowed-out** Full of people, crowded: 'We tried to get into The Scotia but it was stowed-out.'

striped face A graphic description of a face that bears scars: 'You wantin a striped face, pal? Well, shut it then.'

student tobacco A slang term for marijuana, arising from the alleged fondness for it of those involved in higher education, although its consumption is hardly exclusive to them: 'The wee brother hardly ever takes a drink. He's more inty the student tobacco, ye know?'

stupit-lookin An abusive adjective popular among those who prefer not to swear: 'Ach, Ah wish she wid fling that stupit-lookin MP3 player in the bin!' 'Gaun, ya stupit-lookin daft big clown, ye!'

sub A slang term for a boot: 'Ah wis sure Ah left ma subs under the bed.' **To sub** someone or **put the sub on** him is to kick him: 'It wis a clean enough game till their sweeper put the sub on wee Charlie.'

sub crawl A kind of pub crawl that is exclusive to Glasgow, consisting of an attempt to travel round the subway line, getting off at each of the fifteen stations and having a drink in the nearest pub before getting back on. Not recommended.

Subway Like New Yorkers, Glaswegians call the Underground railway **the Subway**. This reflects its original name, the Glasgow District Subway, and resists all official attempts to promote the term Underground: 'We'll get the Subway tae St Enoch an walk it fae there.' 'Last time Ah seen um he wis sellin *The Big Issue* ootside Bridge Street Subway.'

Suckie A nickname for Sauchiehall Street: 'They stay up the far end a Suckie, near the Eye Infirmary.'

Sufferin General A waggish nickname for the Southern General Hospital: 'Is she in the Vicky?' 'Naw, the Sufferin General.'

sugarollie-water A term applied by drinkers to any brew they consider to be insipid or over-sweet: 'How can ye drink sugarollie-water like this when they've got perfectly good export on draught?'

The literal meaning is a drink formerly made by children by shaking up pieces of sugarollie (licorice) in a container of water.

sumdy A local pronunciation of *somebody*: 'Ah hink there sumdy at the door.'

supper No matter what the time of day, any dish sold at a chip-shop that consists of an item with chips is called a **supper**. Thus, a **pie supper** is a pie and chips, a **fish supper** is fish and chips, a **pakora supper** is pakora and chips, and so on: 'Run down tae Elio's an get us a pizza supper, two single fishes, three bars a choclit, an a big boatle a skoosh . . . any kind as long as it's diet.'

sure When someone wants someone else to confirm a statement he often frames a question using this: 'Sure it wis me that went fur the papers yersterday, Da?' 'It's no her that's tae get the first shot, sure it's no?'

swally (rhymes with *tally*) A local variant of *swallow*: 'Sumdy get a haud ae that dug afore it swallies the baw.' **The swally** is a slang term for alcoholic drink: 'He's a wee bit too fond a the swally, that guy.' **A swally** can mean a drink or a drinking session: 'Who's fur a wee swally the morra night?'

swatch (rhymes with *match*) This means a look, especially a brief one, at something: 'Gie's another wee swatch at the instructions.'

sweary word An obscene or offensive word: 'Yer mammy'll no like that book. Too many sweary words in it.'

Sweaty Betty A legendary Glasgow female character troubled by problem perspiration: 'See this heat? Look at the oxturn o this dress . . . Sweaty Betty's no in it!'

This lady is often accompanied by her equally mythical pal Hairy Mary.

swedger A slang word for a sweet: 'Whit gaunet et aw the swedgers?'

sweeties The Scots word for confectionery turns up in several local expressions. Someone who feels he is underpaid in his job may complain of **workin for sweeties**.

Similarly, low wages are often referred to as **sweetie-money**: 'Ye're workin for sweetie-money in there. Ye'd be better aff on the Old King Cole.'

Someone who is very fond of confectionery can be labelled **sweetie-face**: 'Put the chocolates by before wee Sweetie-face comes in.'

sweetie-wife The original meaning of this is a lady who keeps a sweet-shop, but it is often applied to any gossipy person, even a man: 'Ye canny get away fae him if he starts talkin tae ye, the aul sweetie-wife that he is.'

swimmies A familiar term for swimming gear: 'Don't forget yer swimmies the morra.'

swings A shot on the swings literally means a turn on a children's swing, but is used in slang to mean the sexual act: 'Good weekend was it? D'ye get a shot on the swings, aye?'

Time that wean wis walkin.
She's a ton weight.

tackety boots Hobnailed boots, studded on the soles with *tackets*: 'Aw the young lassies are gaun aboot wi big tackety boots on.'

taddie A familiar term for tadpole: 'Sure them wee black things are taddies, granda?'

tail The phrase **on your tail** means on your person, in your possession and usually refers to cash: 'Ah'm no gauny get very far wi wan-fifty oan ma tail, am Ah?'

take This is used in a local construction whereby people are not smitten by or afflicted with something undesirable but **take** it: 'The guy in front of me in the bus queue took a bad turn.' 'She hasny been ower the door since she took a bad back again.' 'If ye carry on like this ye'll take a heart attack.'

A not uncommon threat is **I'll take my hand off your jaw.** This means that the hand will rebound violently from your face, not that it has been lingering there already.

To **take in stairs** means to accept payment for washing other people's stairs in a tenement building, usually on the

163

spot rather than, as the term might suggest, taking them away to do at home.

Tally A local term for Italian: 'The real Tally ice cream's aye the best.' **Tally's blood** is a picturesque if rather old-fashioned nickname for the raspberry sauce often poured over ice cream.

A **Tally Van** is a name sometimes given to an ice-cream van.

tallyman A slang word for a moneylender or loan shark: 'Ah'm inty the tallyman fur two hunner.' Presumably the name comes from the moneylender keeping a tally of how much he is owed by whom.

tan This word is used locally in various ways. It can mean to use something up quickly ('We ferr tanned that haut-boatle') or work briskly at it ('If we tan these last few orders we'll get away early the night'). It can also mean to break something: 'Some bastart's tanned the windscreen oan ma motor.'

To tan a house is to burgle it: 'The polis says it's young boays that's tannin aw the hooses roon here.'

Tanics *or* **Tannies** Nicknames for the Botanic Gardens in the West End: 'It wis a crackin day the day. The Tanics were full a punters sunbathin.'

tank **To tank** someone is to defeat him convincingly: 'We'll tank yeez in the next round.' **A tanking** is an example of this: 'Your lot took a right tankin yesterday.'

To tank also means to move very fast, especially in a motor vehicle: 'Did ye see that fire engine tankin up the road a minute ago?'

In slang use, one's **tank** can mean all the money one has on one's person: 'Ah've got a fiver an some mince an that's ma tank.'

taste In a similar way to **smell**, this is used to mean taint, or give something a flavour of something else, usually undesirable: 'Put that milk in the fridge while Ah'm paintin or the paint'll taste it.'

tea If someone tells you **your tea's oot**, if you're lucky this simply means that a cup of tea has been poured out for you or your evening meal is on the table. Used in a metaphorical manner, the phrase means you are in trouble and should get ready to face the music: 'Yer tea's oot, pal. See me roon the back in two minutes.'

A **teaboy** is an insulting name to call someone who sucks up to a person in authority, implying that he slavishly fetches tea for his master.

team A local term for a gang, as used in certain names like the Govan Team.

Team-handed means accompanied by several friends, especially when expecting trouble: 'Aye, ye're feart tae show yer face roon here unless ye come team-handit, ya crapbag, ye.'

tear (usually pronounced *terr*) This is a spree or any episode involving great enjoyment: 'Yeez were havin a rerr wee terr tae yersels last night, weren't yeez?'

Teddy Bears One of the nicknames for Rangers F.C. or their supporters. This was originally rhyming slang, playing on the local pronunciation of bears as *berrs*, which of course rhymes with *Gers*.

Teddy Bear Country is a nickname for the Ibrox area, home of Rangers' stadium, for those who want to go down to the woods: 'No way am Ah parkin a green motor on a Saturday night in Teddy Bear Country.'

Teenie Teenie fae Troon is a disparaging name applied to any female who presents a hoity-toity image or is much too fancily dressed for her surroundings: 'Wull ye look at Teenie fae Troon ower there! Who does she think she is?'

Teenie Leek is an affectionate name applied to a female child: 'Come on, Teenie Leek, time you were in your bed.'

ten-bob bit Ten bob (shillings) was the pre-decimal equivalent of 50p and is commemorated in this nickname for a fify-pence piece: 'Has emdy got a ten-bob bit fur the meter?'

ten-to-two feet Splayed feet, from the resemblance to the hands of a clock indicating this time: 'That's him there: the big stupit-lookin wan wi the ten-tae-two feet.'

teuchter A mildly disparaging term for a Highlander: 'Her aul man's a teuchter.' 'Ye canny miss that big red teuchter face a his.'

that's A strange, and somewhat redundant, use of the possessive: 'That's mines, but whose is that's?'

there Like *here* this is often used on its own where a verb would normally follow: 'There a big wasp in the lavvy.' 'There ma taxi noo.' 'There only two ae us comin.'

thingmy, thingmyjig, thingwy These words are used as a substitute for the proper names, temporarily forgotten, of something or someone: 'Ah got wee Mrs Thingmy up the road.' 'Gie's another wan a they thingwies.'

this is me Not a redundant introduction of oneself, but part of a description of one's circumstances: 'This is me since yesterday, nuthin tae eat.' 'Ma watter's still cut aff. This is me since last Friday!'

Thistle, the A nickname for Partick Thistle F.C.: 'Fancy gaun tae the Thistle game for a wee change?'

thorn A slang word, particularly in the building trade, for a nail: 'See's ower a handful a thorns, wull ye?'

thought A **thought** is used to mean anything unpleasant or requiring real force of will to face or accomplish: 'It's a thought havin to go back to that big empty house on my own.'

'Tic, the A nickname for Celtic F.C., handy for headline writers on sports pages: ''TIC RAP REF.'

ticket A slang word for a person. A **hard ticket** is someone who acts or looks tough: 'Ah wouldny argue wi a hard ticket like that.' A **useless ticket** is a person considered as good for nothing or shiftless: 'He lies in his bed hauf the day, useless ticket that he is!'

　　To **fancy your ticket** is to have a high opinion of yourself or your chances at something: 'He really fancies his ticket at fitba commentatin.'

tim To **tim** a container, especially one holding liquid, is to empty it: 'Tim thae cups inty the sink, will ye?' 'He timt the hale boatle doon the stank.'

Tim A nickname for any Roman Catholic, apparently short-ened from *Tim Malloy*, although whether this was an actual individual or represents a kind of generic Irish name I have not been able to discover: 'She married a Tim, your sister, didn't she?'

A chapel is sometimes referred to as a **Timshop**.

toe-ender A kick, using the point of the boot: 'You call it a well-placed shot an I say it was nothin but a jammy toe-ender.' 'Oot ma road or ye'll get a toe-ender up yer jacksy.'

toley A local word for the product of a bowel movement. Like many such terms it is often used as a name to call some one objectionable: 'Gie the wumman a break, ya miserable wee toley!'

ton weight A term applied to anything, including people, considered to be too heavy: 'Time that wean wis walkin. She's a ton weight.'

tore Someone who energetically sets about a person or thing is often said to **get tore in**: 'Ah'm gaun roon there this minute tae get tore inty the bampot.' 'Get tore right inty they samosas afore they get cauld.'

torn-faced A term applied to someone who looks miserable or aggrieved, especially if this is his habitual expression: 'That social worker Ah had tae see was a right torn-faced bisom.'

toss *or* **tossbag** An insulting name: 'What're *you* sayin, ya toss?' The suggestion is that the person insulted is given to self-abuse.

tosser Most often found in the phrase **not worth a tosser**, this literally means a coin of low value, such as a penny used in games of pitch and toss: 'That video you selt us isny worth a tosser.' 'Ah don't gie a tosser what you think.'

totty A local word for a potato: 'Gie's a baked totty an chili.'

To say that someone is **no the clean totty** is to suggest that he is involved in dishonest activities. Presumably this is a comparison to a potato that still has dirt sticking to it.

A **totty-muncher is** a derogatory name for an Irish person, and hence anyone of Irish descent, from the idea of the potato being the staple diet of Ireland. It is also extended to apply to any Catholic or Celtic supporter.

A **totty-peelin** accent or voice is one considered posh or affected: 'She jist puts on that totty-peelin voice when she answers the phone.'

A **totty scone** is a potato scone: 'Ah'll just have one of yer totty scones cold, wi a wee bit butter on it.'

A woman wearing clothes that emphasise her plumpness is often compared to a **bag of totties**: 'Ah'm like a bag a totties in this dress noo.'

toty A term applied to anything very small or a person very young: 'Aw! Look at these wee toty shoes!' 'Ye said he wisny tall but ye never said he wis toty!'

trackie A tracksuit: 'Kin Ah get a Scotland trackie fur ma Christmas?'

trackie bottoms are the lower half of a tracksuit, adopted as casual wear for all occasions: 'Mammy! She's away oot in ma trackie bottoms an she never even asked us!'

trainies A local term for training shoes: 'The boay wants sixty notes fur a new perr a trainies.'

troubles Someone who is beset by difficulties may have it said of him that he **doesn't have his troubles to seek**: 'She's no got her troubles tae seek since she got mixed up wi that useless ticket.'

trouble-the-hoose A title given to any young baby whose crying and urgent needs inevitably disturb the peace of a household: 'See's ower wee Trouble-the-hoose till ye get a cup a tea.'

tube A stupid or contemptible person: 'Yer bum's oot the windy, ya tube, ye!'

tummle Tumble. To **tummle yer wilkies** is to do a somersault: 'Wait till ye see the wean tummlin his wilkies.' This apparently comes from the idea of tumbling like wildcats.

To take a **tummle to yourself** is to see the error of one's ways, smarten up one's thinking or behaviour: 'Ye better take a tummle tae yersel or ye'll be gettin yer jotters.'

tumshie A turnip. The word is often used as an insult implying stupidity: 'How d'ye expect the kettle tae boil when it's no even plugged in, ya tumshie?' A stupid person may also be referred to as **tumshie-heid**.

tuppence The sum of two pennies in pre-decimal money, still heard in popular idioms. For example, a small child may be described as being no the size a tuppence.

No **worth tuppence** can mean that something so described is of little value, or, when applied to a person, that they are exhausted: 'Ah'm no worth tuppence efter Ah've come up they stairs.'

turkey Someone who eats a great deal at a sitting may be said to **stuff his turkey**: 'D'ye mean tae say you've been sittin here stuffin yer turkey while Ah've been oot graftin?'

turn A turn is a win at gambling, perhaps reflecting the punter's necessary faith that everyone gets a chance to be lucky: 'Ah see Joe's had a turn. Away an nip him fir a twinty.'

twally (rhymes with *Sally*) An idiot: 'Ah said no tae drap your end till Ah telt ye, ya twally!'

twicet A local form of *twice*: 'She's been wanst an Ah've been twicet.'

two-up The **two-up** is the offensive V-sign made with two fingers: 'Dae you let yer wee boay away wi giein folk the two-up?'

Ye jist cannae be up tae um!

um In broad Glaswegian speech, a version of *him*: 'If Ah get um Ah'm gauny stiffen um.'

Uni Short for University, of which Glasgow now has more than it used to. **The Uni** tends to mean the University of Glasgow in particular: 'He's managed to get a flat up near the Uni.'

up In the field of gambling, to describe something as **up** means that it has won: 'Maybe we'll have the coupon up this week.' 'That's me got a line up.'

    The phrase **up the toon** means into the city centre: 'Ah'm away up the toon fur a new jaiket.'

    Ye canny be up tae um is said of someone, especially a mischievous child, whose behaviour is impossible to predict: 'Ah sent um inty the hoose cause he wis pullin up ma daffadils, an when Ah went in he wis feedin the baby a dug biscuit . . . ye jist canny be up tae um!'

ur A local version of *are*: 'Ye're a great wee soul, so ye ur!'

urny The negative of the above, *aren't*. 'Ye urny much good at this, ur ye?' 'We urny getting away early at aw.'

He used tae work in Pearson's in Vicky Road, feedin the parrot...

verse This means to play against someone in a game: 'Away in an get yer baw an Ah'll verse ye at heidies.' This odd expression comes from the term *versus* (as in 'Pollok versus Rob Roy') being understood as if it was a verb *verses*.

vicky The **vicky** is the rude two-fingered V-sign: 'He got sent off for givin the fans the vicky.' The term is probably shortened from *victory*, as in the V-sign popularised during the Second World War by Winston Churchill.

Vicky, the A familiar name for the Victoria Infirmary: 'She's got that much wrong with her she's got a season ticket for the Vicky.'

Vicky Road A familiar name for Victoria Road, a main business and shopping thoroughfare on the South Side: 'He used tae work in Pearson's in Vicky Road, feedin the parrot.'

voddy Vodka, or a measure of this: 'She's tanned a hale boatle a voddy hersel.' 'Gie's two voddies . . . wan wi lime in it.'

Right intae the wid...

wacky baccy A slang term for marijuana: 'What are you gigglin at? Been at the wacky baccy or somethin?'

wae In broad Glaswegian speech, a version of *with*: 'If yeez ur aw gaun Ah'm comin wae yeez.'

Walk, the The name by which most people refer to the Orange Walk, held each year on the Saturday nearest to the twelfth of July: 'We were held up for ages with the Walk goin along the Paisley Road.'

To **break the Walk** is to cross the street in front of the main body of the parade or through a gap between bands; not likely to endear one to the marchers.

There are other minor Orange marches in the summer, before the main one, and these are known as **wee walks**.

wallies (pronounced to rhyme with *valleys*) This means false teeth: 'If Ah've tae spend any mair on fillins Ah'm gauny get that dentist tae rip the hale jing-bang oot an gie us a set a wallies.' The term suggests that the false teeth might be made of china, or *wally*, as it is called in Scots.

Wallies is also a collective term for a very small sum of money, especially poor wages: 'Ye get paid wallies in that place.' The origin of this might be the former childhood use of bits of broken china as play-money.

walloper (pronounced with the *a* as in *ballot*) A slang term for the penis.

wally (rhymes with *valley*) This means made from china or porcelain. A **wally dug** is an ornament in the form of a china dog: 'Look at the two of them sittin at both ends of the settee like a pair a wally dugs.'

A **wally close** is a close in a tenement building that has china tiles on its walls rather than just paint, considered a sign of poshness: 'That last flat we looked at was the best . . . a wally close an aw!'

The **wally waw**, literally porcelain wall, is a slang term for a gents' urinal of the kind consisting of one complete porcelain receptacle running the length of a wall: 'Ach well, Ah'll need tae go an staun at the wally waw.'

Someone who is described as having a **wally heid** is considered simple-minded, not right in the head. Similarly, to call someone **wally-heid** shows that you think he is a simpleton.

Wally Dishes, the A nickname for St Aloysius College, a secondary school in Garnethill. A clever play on Aloysius and *wally* in the sense of china.

wan A local term for *one*: 'At wan's mines.' 'Ah'll get ye at hauf wan.'

wance Once: 'Ah only went the wance.'

wancer A local version of the slang term *oncer*, meaning £1, especially a pound note: 'Ah wouldny gie ye a wancer fur the perr a them.'

wanner *or* **wanny** To do something **in a wanner** or **wanny** is to do it in one go: 'He horsed back his pint in a wanner.'

To wanner a person is to give him a single destructive punch: 'Wee Eddie just walked right up tae the guy an wannered um.'

174

wanst A local term for *once*: 'Wanst I had a secret lo-ove . . .'

wap (rhymes with *cap*) A multipurpose word, somewhat ono-matopoeic. It can mean to hit: 'She wapped him wan ower the heid.' Or a blow: 'It's only a bluebottle . . . gie it a wap wi the paper.' It can also be a sound effect: 'Ah beltit roon the coarner – wap! – right inty this big bear!'

warmer (sometimes pronounced to rhyme with *farmer*) This is a word for an exasperating or despicable person: 'He wouldny gie the weans their baw back when it went inty his garden, the aul warmer that he is!'

washers (pronounced to rhyme with *rashers*) This is a dispar-aging term for small change: 'When Ah asked ye for change of a pound Ah wis hopin for two fifties, no a pile a washers.'

waste To **waste** a thing or person is to spoil it or them: 'Don't let the dug jump up on the new settee or she'll waste it.' To **waste someone's face** is to disfigure it by violence: 'If he comes that crack wi me Ah'll waste his face for him.'

A **wastit** person, especially a child, is someone who has been spoiled by being over-indulged: 'Weans nooadays are wastit wi aw their mobile phones an DVDs an aw that.' 'Can you no act lik a grown man instead of a big wastit wean?' A person who looks sulky may be called **wastit-face**.

Someone whose **heid's wastit** is stupid, distracted, or sim-ply too tired to think properly: 'Never mind askin that big stumer . . . his heid's wastit.' 'Ah'm tryin tae think of a phone number, but ma heid's wastit after the day Ah've had.'

watchie A familiar term for a watchman: 'Ye'd think the watchie would check they weans for playin on that buildin site.'

watter Water. To go **doon the watter** is a traditional Glasgow phrase which mean to take a pleasure-cruise down the river and Firth of Clyde to various resorts such as Millport, Rothesay or Largs.

way **On yer way!** is of course a phrase used to tell someone to leave, but in some contexts, such as at a football game, it can be a cry of encouragement: 'On yer way, big yin! Take the lot a them on yersel!'

wean (pronounced *wayne*) The local term, as opposed to the more easterly *bairn*, for a baby or child: 'Ah'll need tae go an get the weans fae school.' 'She's another wean on the road.' 'They've only got weans' sizes left in that shoe.' A **big wean** is a grown-up who is acting childishly: 'He's gauny start greetin in a minute, the big wean!'

weanish means like or suitable for a child, often meant as a criticism: 'D'ye no think he's getting a bit big fur weanish toys like that?'

weather The phrase **this weather** is used to mean at this time, or these days: 'How's yer aul faither keepin this weather?'

wee The Scots word for *small* is used to mean younger: 'Ma wee brother an ma wee cousin're comin round.'

   Wee-er means smaller or younger: 'Ye'll need a wee-er screw than that.' 'It's only the wee-er weans that're getting oot early.'

   Wee-est means smallest or youngest: 'Who's the wee-est at your Brownies?'

wee boy A term used to mean a perticular individual, especially one who is ideally suited for a specific task: 'That guy needs to be told to mind his own business, an I'm the wee boy to do it!'

wee goldie A familiar name for a glass of whisky, alluding to the drink's golden colour: 'Stick a wee goldie for Auld Walter on the round next time.'

wee mad A pair of adjectives used together to describe practically anything: 'That wee mad teacher keeps giein us homework on a Friday.' 'Ah pure love that wee mad jaikit she's got oan.' This usage seems to have no overtones of either criticism or praise, but is thrown in to any handy phrase just as a kind of verbal adornment.

wee man An affectionate title or form of address for a male child or small adult: 'Have ye skint yer knee, wee man?' 'Hey wee man, ye comin fur a pint?' Not to be confused with this at any cost in the occasional use of this to mean the penis: 'He had his wee man oot!' A **wee man** is often used as a blanket term for any tradesman employed to do specific jobs, irrespective of his actual stature: 'My mother says she'll get a wee man out the local paper to do the garden.'

In the name a the wee man is an expression of surprise, disgust or astonishment: 'In the name a the wee man, wid ye look at the state a them!' 'Jist whit in the name a the wee man were ye tryin tae dae?' Apparently the particular wee man referred to in this case was originally the Devil.

Wee Rangers A nickname for Berwick Rangers F.C., used to distinguish them from Glasgow Rangers.

wee team A familiar term for the reserve team of a football club, the first eleven being the **big team**: 'The big no-user canny even get a game for the wee team.'

well Used in the sense of 'in that case', this turns up at the end rather than the beginning of statements: 'Are ye no wantin that tottie? Gie it tae me, well.'

well-fired Describes baked items, like rolls, loaves or scones, that have been in the oven longer than others and may be almost black on the outside: 'Ye know yer granda likes a well-fired roll in the mornin.'

well-got A local variant of *well in*, being on good terms with: 'Aye, he gets aw the overtime he wants cause he's well-got wi that supervisor.'

wellied Another term meaning *drunk*: 'He wis that wellied he disny even mind me talkin tae him.'

To **get wellied in** means the same as get stuck in, that is, to set about something vigorously: 'Right boys, let's get wellied inty this carry-out.'

well on In an advanced state of inebriation: 'Wan look at her an ye could see she wis well on already.'

well seen Plain, patently obvious, to be expected: 'There was some queue for petrol. It's well seen there's a Budget today.'

welly As a verb this means to kick powerfully: 'Celtic areny a team tae just welly it up the park an chase it.'

went Used where others would say *gone*: 'He hasny went back since.' If someone says 'The door went' this doesn't mean that it has independently parted company with its hinges and disappeared, but rather that there was a knock or ring at the door. The same applies to telephones, bells, sirens, etc.: 'We'll make it. The bell hasny went yet.'

West-Endie An inhabitant of Glasgow's West End, an area roughly west of Charing Cross, north of Argyle Street, south of Maryhill Road and shading away westwards to the far suburbs. This is its geography, but some would say it is more a state of mind. It is the famous stamping ground of students (real and pretendy ones), artists and writers (ditto) and fashionables. The fuller form of the term, **trendy West-Endie**, gives an idea of how this sub-culture is often viewed in other parts of the city: 'This used tae be a real workin-man's pub. Noo it's full a West-Endies an heid-the-baws makin documentaries.'

Western, the To say that somebody is 'in the Western' is not to imply a role in a cowboy film but that the individual concerned is an in-patient of the Western Infirmary.

whack The phrase **not the full whack** means incomplete, not up to scratch, below par: 'Are you feelin okay? Ye're not lookin the full whack the day at all.'
   For **cop your whack** see under **cop**.

what The phrase **what is it?** is a common way of asking someone what he wants to drink. Another similar question is **what are you on?** which can also (when emphasis is put on *on*) be an implication that the person addressed has done or said something so ridiculous that he must be drunk or high on drugs: 'Ye did what? What are you *on*, pal?'

wheech (pronounced with the *ch* as in *loch*) This means to move (or move something) away at great speed: 'We'll jump in the motor an wheech down to Largs for the day.' 'Ah'd just taken wan bite oot ma piece an put it doon fur a minute when that dampt dug came up an wheeched it.'

wheesht To **haud yer wheesht** means to keep quiet, refrain from talking: 'Would youse lot haud yer wheesht till we hear what the man's sayin?' **Wheesht!** is a command to be silent.

whitey *or* **white-oot** To **take a whitey** or **white-oot** means to suddenly turn very pale because of feeling sick or dizzy: 'See that boay takin a whitey? Get him oot inty the close away fae ma good carpet.'

wick A **wick** is an annoying or bad-natured person: 'Leave yer wee brither alane, ya wee wick, ye!'

wid¹ A local variant of *would*: 'Wid ye credit it?' The negative of this is **widny**: 'Ah widny dae that tae emdy.'

wid² A local variant of *wood*; 'Ah canny go that French bread it's lik chewin a dod a wid.'

Someone who has had a very short haircut may have it described as **right inty the wid**.

Widden means made of wood, wooden: 'Ye're better wi an iron gate than a widden wan.'

wide To **make someone wide** is to let him in on some useful information, put him wise to the facts: 'Ah knew this wis comin aff. Big Dan made us wide tae it the other night.'

A **wide member** is a flyman (see **wido**).

wido *or* **wide-oh** A slang term for a rogue, criminal or flyman: 'The only folk that drink in here are neds, chancers, hardmen an widos. Whit wan are you?'

wilkies For **tummle yer wilkies** see under **tummle**.

willn't, willny Two local versions of *will not* or *won't*: 'He says he'll come but I know he willn't.'

Wilma A nickname for a female Protestant, especially a Rangers supporter, being a female form of *William*.

winch To **winch** is to kiss and cuddle: 'They were winchin in the back row at the pictures.' It also means to go out regularly with someone of the opposite sex, to date him or her: 'Her Mary an oor Jason have been winchin for ages.' The question 'Are ye winchin?' is often asked of young people by elders who wish to embarrass them, meaning 'Are you going out with someone?'

windy *or* **windae** A local word for *window*: 'Shut that windy, or the budgie'll be aff its mark.'

If something is described as being **out the windy** this means that it is no longer possible: 'We were gauny get a new fittit kitchen till he lost his job an that wis that oot the windy.'

Yer bum's oot the windy means 'You are talking nonsense'. I suppose the suggestion is that what you are saying is so outrageously silly that you should be as embarrassed to be heard saying it as you would be if you were making a public exhibition of your posterior.

Wine City A disparaging nickname for the Greenock/Port Glasgow conurbation, deriving from the Glaswegian belief that the natives thereof yield to no others as champion consumers of cheap strong wine.

wine-mopper A disparaging term for someone who drinks a lot of fortified cheap wine, especially a down-and-out: 'You're gauny end up sleepin on Glesga Green wi the rest a the wine-moppers.' It is sometimes shortened to **mopper**.

wineshop A slang term for a pub that specialises in selling cheap strong wine by the glass: 'Naw, we don't stock that in here. It's a wineshop you're wantin, aul yin, no a wine bar.'

wired If a person is described as **wired up but no plugged in** this means he is not right in the head.

An individual who is slightly crazy or abnormally energetic may be described as being **wired to the moon**. Another version of this is **wired to a Mars Bar**.

wise A person described as being **not wise** or **no wise** is considered gullible: 'Ye canny be expected tae agree tae that! D'ye want people tae think ye're no wise?'

wiss A slang term for urination: 'Ah'll just dive in fur a wiss.'

workie A familiar term for a workman: 'There's a gang of workies digging up the street.'

worky up In children's talk this concerns playground swings, meaning to get your swing going from a standing start up to the speed and height of arc desired: 'You sit on the swing next to me an I'll show ye how to worky up.'

wrap it To stop doing something, or cancel something: 'If Ah don't win somethin on the lottery soon Ah'm fur wrappin it.' 'When he said it would take another three weeks for delivery I told him just to wrap the whole thing.' **Wrap it!** is used to command someone to stop talking.

wulk A local variation of *whelk*: 'Eatin a bag a wulks wi a pin.' To **howk yer wulk** is to pick your nose, presumably comparing this activity with prising a whelk out of its their shell.

Full as a whelk is another term for drunk, implying, I suppose, that the person so described can no sooner swallow any more drink than a shell with a whelk in it can contain anything else.

wulln't, wullny Broad Glaswegian versions of *willn't* and *willny*: 'The wean wullny eat chicken.'

wummin A woman: 'There a picture of a big bare wummin on the front a that video.'

Mrs Wummin is a name used to address or refer to a woman who is unknown to the speaker: 'Haw! Mrs Wummin! It's you next.'

wur A broad Glaswegian term for *our*: 'Where ur we gaun fur wur hoalidays this year?'

wursels Ourselves: 'Just when we're beginnin tae enjoy wursels we've tae go hame.'

X, Y &

Big zeds.

-y The word *of* in broad Glasgow speech often comes out sounding like a *y* added to the end of the word it follows: 'Gie us somey they crisps.' 'Ah'm fed up wi the pairy yeez.'

ya bass An expression originally found in gang slogans marked on walls, as in 'Pollok Crew ya bass', which I assume is meant to be a punchier version of 'you bastard'. The phrase crossed over into more common use as part of any bombastic or defiant statement: 'Govan Initiative rule, ya bass!'

yabber To talk idly, chatter: 'Ah canny concentrate on ma crossword wi aw yer yabberin.'

yap An extemely talkative or gossipy person: 'That wee yap would talk the hind legs off a donkey.'

ye A form of *you* which is often appended to an insult, magnifying and focussing its stength: 'Ya stupit-lookin monkey, ye!'
   The plural for is **yeez**: 'If yeez think yeez're onty a cushy number here yeez've got another think comin.'

yelp A term for a child that is continually whingeing or being cheeky: 'An that lassie a theirs is a right wee yelp an aw.'

yin A form of *one* that in Glasgow speech is only used as the object of a statement: 'Ah'll have that yin there.' It is often used to refer to people, particularly in tandem with an adjective describing the person: **auld yin, big yin, wee yin, young yin**.

The plural is **yins**: 'These yins are the best.' This often turns up in combinations, referring to people as a group: **them yins, youse yins, us yins**.

yon time A term used to mean an undetermined but far too late hour: 'Are we expected to hang around this place till yon time?'

yop A school term meaning to clype, tell on someone: 'Ah hink Ah know who yopped on us.' Someone who does this is a **yop** or **yopper**.

yous Used to address more than one person at the same time: 'Any a yous got a light?'

y's A slang term for male underpants: 'Ah canny find a clean pair a y's.'

yuck it A Glasgow variant of *chuck it*, that is, stop it: 'Yuck it yous, or Ah'm tellin on yeez.'

yumyum A cake highly popular in Glasgow, whose citizens of course yield to no-one in the field of teeth-destroying sweet things. For those who don't know, it is similar in consistency to a doughnut, but is oblong rather than round and is sometimes twisted in the middle: 'Ah canny make up ma mind between yumyums an empire biscuits.'

zed To **have a few zeds** and **stack up some zeds** are slang expressions meaning to have a sleep. **Big zeds** means a long deep sleep, as opposed to forty winks: 'Ah'm definitely needin big zeds the night. Ma eyes are hingin oot ma heid.'

The origin of this is the children's comics convention of showing that a character is asleep by inserting a string of zeds where a speech bubble would normally go.

Rhyming slang

A lot of rhyming slang is used in everyday Glasgow speech, not all of which was coined there. In this compilation I have tried to include only examples that are genuinely Glaswegian in origin, even if some of them have gone on to achieve a wider currency.

One of the factors that make rhyming slang unintelligible to the uninitiated is that individual expressions often consist of two words, with the second part, which gives the rhyme, often being unspoken but understood by hearers who are in the know. Because of this I list my items in alphabetical order according to the first word, in the hope that the reader will find the meaning of an expression suspected to be rhyming slang even if only the first part has been heard.

Abraham Lincoln Stinkin: 'Your plates are Abraham Lincoln!'

acme wringers Fingers. the fact that this rhymes is an illustration of the local pronunciation of fingers. An Acme Wringer I assume to be a proprietary brand of clothes wringer.

Arthur Lowe No, a negative answer: 'Fancy another?' 'Ah wouldny say arthur.' Arthur Lowe (1915-82) was, of course, a household name as the star of several popular TV comedy series of the 1970s, such as *Dad's Army*.

Bayne and Ducket A bucket, using the name of a well-known chain of shoe shops. Sometimes used as an exclamation, substituting for something a good deal stronger.

Bertie Auld Cauld, that is, cold: 'It's turned a wee bit Bertie noo.' Bertie Auld is famous as a member of the Celtic Lisbon Lions side.

Bengal Lancer A chancer: 'Whit's that big Bengal sayin noo?'

Carolina China, meaning a friend. This is an example of one piece of rhyming slang standing for another, as *china* in this sense is also rhyming slang (china plate = mate).

Charles Laughton Rotten: 'The smell in here is pure Charles Laughton!' The man referred to (1899-1962) was, of course, a famous English film actor.

Chic Murray The late and much lamented droll comedian's name is taken in vain to mean a curry.

chorus an verse Erse, i.e. arse: 'Just you sit on yer chorus an shut up!'

collie dug Mug, i.e. a fool: 'They're makin me look a right collie dug!'

corn(ed) beef Deef, i.e. deaf: 'Ye'll need tae speak up a bit, hen. Ah'm a wee bit corned beef.' Sometimes shortened to **corny**.

Cowdenbeath Teeth: 'Ah'll just run the brush roon the aul Cowdenbeath then Ah'm inty ma scratcher.'

cream bun Hun, i.e. a Protestant.

cream cookie A bookie, including his premises or betting shop: 'Away doon the cream cookie an lift what's lyin fur this line.'

cream puff Huff: 'He's no talkin tae us noo . . . he's took the cream puff.'

Crossmyloof Poof, i.e. male homosexual. Crossmyloof is an area of the South Side formerly famous for its ice rink.

currant bun A nun.

Dan Dares Flares, i.e. flared trousers; after the spaceman hero of the *Eagle* comic: 'Ah see the Dan Dares are comin back inty fashion.'

deedle doddle Model, i.e. Model Lodging House (see **model** in main text).

dirty beast A priest.

disco dancer A chancer: 'He's a bitty a disco dancer, that pal a yours, eh?'

dolly dimple Simple, in the sense of not very clever: 'Ye'll need tae excuse her . . . she's a wee bit dolly.'

Donald Duck Luck. Often shortened to **donald**: 'If there's nae tickets left when ye get there it's just yer donald.'

Duke of Argylls Piles, i.e. haemorrhoids: 'He's a martyr tae the Duke a Argylls, so he is.'

Duke of Montrose Nose.

Easter egg Beg, as in **on the Easter egg,** begging for money: 'Never mind comin roon here on the Easter egg, ya aul moocher, ye!'

Elsie Tanner A wanner, i.e. a single complete action or example: 'Whit d'ye hink? Another coat a mully on the ceilin or lee it wi an Elsie Tanner?' This derives from the name of a well-known former character in the TV soap opera *Coronation Street.*

everlastin joob-joob A tube, i.e. the slang word for an idiot: 'Look at the mess ye're makin, ya everlastin joob-joob!' The term literally means a kind of long-lasting sucking sweetie.

fillet of fish Pish, i.e. urination.

Frankie Vaughans Hauns, i.e. hands. The well-known singer in question (1928-99) was connected with anti-gang youth work in Easterhouse in the 1960s.

Friar Tucked Thwarted.

Garngad Bad: 'How ye getting on the day?' 'No too Garngad.' This is the name of an area in the north of the city and its use reflects the local pronunciation, with the stress on the second syllable.

gas-cookered Snookered, i.e. thwarted, prevented from getting something done: 'If that last nut'll no shift that'll be us gas-cookered.'

gasket jint (*jint* being a local pronunciation of joint, on the model of *jiner,* joiner) A pint, usually of beer: 'Moan we'll nick oot fur a couple a gaskets.'

Gene Tunney Money. This one shows its age when you know that Gene Tunney was an American boxer who was world heavyweight champion 1926-28.

gone an dunnit Bunnit, i.e. a man's flat cap: 'Now, where did I put ma gone and dunnit?'

good looks Books, in the sense of employment documents returned to a sacked worker: 'Carry on like this an ye'll be getting yer good looks.'

Gregory Pecks Specs, i.e. spectacles, glasses: 'Time ah wis getting testit fur a new perr a gregories.' Sometimes shortened to **gregs**: 'Aw naw! Now Ah've lost ma gregs!'

Hampden Roar Score, as used in the question, 'What's the score?' meaning what's going on, what's the story?: 'What's the Hampden Roar wi aw this shoutin an bawlin?'

ham sandwich Language. This only works if you remember that the second part is often pronounced as *sangwidge.* 'Just keep the ham sangwidge respectable in front a ma aul dear, eh?'

happy jack Smack, i.e. the slang word for heroin.

harry hoof Poof, i.e. male homosexual.

Harry Wraggs Jags, which is of course a nickname for Partick Thistle F.C.; 'We're the Jags! Harry Wraggs!' The individual whose name is borrowed here was a famous racing jockey and trainer in the 1930s.

haw maw In the singular this can mean a saw: 'See's ower the big haw maw.' In the plural it means baws, i.e. testicles: 'Ooyah! Right in the haw maws!' 'Ye've made a right haw maws a this.'

The expression **haw maw** is itself a cry to attract the attention of one's mother.

hey-diddle-diddle Fiddle, in the sense of a swindle: 'He was caught at the hey-diddle-diddle with the books.'

hi-diddler Fiddler, i.e. violin player: 'There's a hi-diddler giein it laldy in the lounge.'

hillbilly Chilly: 'Ah thought this mornin it wis gauny be nice but it's turned kinna hillbilly noo.'

holy ghost Coast: 'Fancy a wee run doon the holy ghost?'

honey perrs Sterrs, i.e. stairs: 'Ah'm away up the honey perrs.' **Honey Perrs!** meaning sweet pears, was an old street cry of a fruit seller.

hoosie Fraser House of Fraser, the department-store company, used here to mean razor. Sometimes shortened to **hoosie** (rhymes with *Lucy*).

hot peas Knees.

iron lung Bung, i.e. a tip or gratuity: 'The moolly aul get never even gied us an iron lung.'

Jack an Jill The Pill: 'She's wantin tae come aff the Jack.'

Jack Dash A slash, i.e. urination: 'Ah'll just have a quick Jack Dash then we're off.'

jaggy nettle Kettle: 'Stick the jaggy on for a coffee.'

jeely jar Car: 'This the new jeely jar, eh?'

Jock Mackay A pie, usually taken to mean a Scotch pie: 'Ah had a couple a Jock Mackays fur ma tea.' This mythical person also turns up in an expression said as a sigh: 'Och aye, Jock Mackay!'

Joe Baxi A taxi: 'Never mind the motor. We'll dive inty a Joe Baxi.' Apparently, this comes from the name of a famous American boxer of the 1940s, Joe Baksi.

Joe Loss Gloss, i.e. gloss paint: 'We'll need another coupla gallon a Joe Loss.' The original Joe Loss (1909-90) was a famous English bandleader.

Joe the Toff Off, i.e. away, gone, on one's way: 'Right, that's me Joe the Toff. Cheerybyes!'

John Greigs Legs: 'A fine perr a John Greigs.' The man referred to is, of course, a famous Rangers player of the 1960s and 70s.

Jungle Jim Tim, i.e. a Roman Catholic: 'Just cause ye've got an Irish name doesny mean ye're a Jungle Jim.'

kelly bow Dough, i.e. money: 'Ah'd get ye a pint but Ah'm kinna light on the kelly bow at the moment.'

Kenneth Mackellar Cellar.

kirby grips Chips: 'Gauny get us a bag a kirby grips?'

Legal Aid Lemonade: 'A wee splash a Legal Aid in wan a they haufs, young yin.'

lemon curd Burd, i.e. bird, meaning a young woman, especially one's girlfriend: 'Canny make it the night. It's the lemon curd's birthday.'

Lillian Gish Pish: 'Ah got caught short for a Lilian Gish.' Similarly **Lillian Gished** means pished, i.e. drunk. What a way to commemorate a movie star!

love an romancin Dancin: 'Ma folks are away tae the love an romancin at the community centre.'

Macnamara Barra, i.e. barrow: 'Gie's a haun tae load these bricks inty the Macnamara, wull ye?'

mammy mine Wine: 'He's a wee bit too fond a the mammy mine.'

Manfred Mann Tan, as in suntan: 'She's away doon tae the sunbed tae top up the Manfred Mann.'

man from Cairo Giro, i.e. a benefits payment.

Mars Bar Scar: 'You're lookin for a Mars Bar, pal.'

merry laird Beard (in local pronunciation, *baird* or *berrd*): 'What made ye decide to get rid of the merry laird?'

Mickey Mouse Grouse, i.e. a measure of the Famous Grouse proprietary brand of whisky: 'A Mickey Mouse an a wee heavy, barman.'

Mickey Rooney Loony, i.e. an insane person: 'It's no joke stayin through the waw fae a Mickey Rooney lik that.'

Mick Jagger Lager: 'They Mick Jaggers in the fridge should be Bertie Auld by now.' This only constitutes a rhyme in local pronunciation. In London, for example, *Jagger* and *lager* have different sounds.

Mr Happy A nappy: 'It's definitely your turn to change the wee guy's Mr Happy.' This of course refers to the smiling symbol of the 'Glasgow's Miles Better' campaign of the 1980s.

Moby Dick Sick: 'Haud on a minute. Ah'm feelin a bit Moby.'

mountain goat Coat: 'Ah'm pittin on the mountain goat, case it gets hillbilly later on.'

Nat King Cole Hole, i.e. sexual intercourse: 'He thought he wis gauny get his Nat King.'

Oscar Slater Later: 'Ah'll get ye Oscar Slater.' The name comes from the defendant in a highly controversial murder case in Glasgow in the 1900s.

Paddy McGuigan Jiggin, i.e. dancing: 'We're aw gaun tae the Paddy McGuigan the night.' I take this to refer to a supposedly typical Irish name rather than to any particular individual.

Paddy McGuire A fire: 'Sling another shovel on the Paddy McGuire while ye're up.' The comment on the preceding name also applies here.

pan breid Deid, i.e. dead: 'Ye never telt us yer dug wis pan breid.' Pan bread is, of course, a type of loaf with a light crust all round it.

Pansy Potters Jotters, i.e. documents returned to a dismissed employee: 'She'd only been there a year when they gave her her Pansy Potters.' See under **Pansy Potter** in the main text for an explanation of the name.

paraffin ile (*ile* being a local pronunciation of *oil*) Style: 'Ye never see Wee Jack gaun oot withoot a bit a paraffin aboot him.'

Parkheid smiddies Diddies, i.e. a woman's breasts. This comes from a famous forge in Parkhead, in the city's East End.

Pat and Mick Sick: 'He's huvin a couple a days off on the Pat an Mick.'

pea pod Tod. **On yer pea pod** means **on yer tod**, which means on your own, alone. Like *Carolina*, this is a case of one piece of rhyming slang standing for another, as *tod* is short for Tod Sloan, and **on yer Tod Sloan** is rhyming slang for on your own: 'Are you gauny let her walk up the road on her pea pod?' Tod Sloan, for those who want to know, was a famous American jockey who raced in the UK around the turn of the 20th century.

pearl diver A fiver, i.e. a five pound note: 'Ah fun a pearl diver doon the settee.'

pineapple Chapel. The stress of the pronunciation goes on the second part of the word, i.e. pine*apple*: 'Yer mammy's away up the pineapple.'

pot of glue Clue: 'He hasny got a pot, the stumer that he is.'

pottit heid Deid, i.e. deceased: 'Ah think yer goldfish is pottit heid.' Potted head is, of course, a traditional Scots delicacy made from a sheep's head.

radio rental Mental, i.e. insane: 'The guy's totally radio, Ah'm tellin ye.'

rooty-ma-toot A suit: 'Should ah put on the rooty-ma-toot for this do?'

Rossy Docks Socks: 'Ah'm huntin fur a clean pair a Rossy Docks.' **Rossy** is of course the local pronunciation of *Rothesay*, and the Rothesay Dock was a dock on the north bank of the Clyde near Yoker.

St Louis blues News: 'Bung on the telly till we get the St Louis blues.'

Salvador Dali Swally, i.e. swallow, meaning drink: 'Gie us a bell next time ye're up for a Salvador Dali.' The famous Spanish surrealist's name is well known in Glasgow through the prominence in the Kelvingrove Gallery's collection of his iconic painting *Christ of St John of the Cross*.

satin and silk Milk: 'We'll have a cup a tea when the wean comes back wi the satin an silk.'

scooby doo Clue. See **scooby** in main text.

shammy leather A blether.

single fish Pish: 'Ah'll need tae go fur a single fish.' 'Well, get us a pie supper.'

skin diver A fiver.

soapy bubble Trouble: 'Tell yer mate he's in deep soapy.'

song an dancer Chancer: 'Ah widny trust that big song an dancer as far as Ah could boot um.'

south of the border Out of order, meaning unacceptable, not the done thing in terms of behaviour: 'Here, is that no a wee bit south of the border whit he's sayin?'

    The border referred to is that between the United States and Mexico, rather than Scotland and England, an example of the Glaswegian love for and identification with the Western movie.

tackety bits (literally hobnailed boots) Tits. Often shortened to **tacketies**: 'That's a fine perr a tacketies on that wee thing.'

taury rope Tarry rope, i.e. the Pope: 'When wis it the aul taury rope wis at Bellahouston Park?'

teedle-ee A pee, i.e. urination: 'He'll no be long. He's just away for a teedle-ee.' I would take this as coming from deedling, that is, singing meaningless words in imitation of music played by a band.

tin flute A suit; 'Ye better wear the tin flute for yer interview.'

Tommy Trotter A snotter: 'Ye've a wee Tommy Trotter at yer nose.'
   I don't know if this refers to an actual person, but it's hardly the nicest way to be immortalised.

varicose veins Weans.

wine grape Pape, i.e. a Roman Catholic: 'It's aw wine grapes that drink in there.'

winners an losers Troosers, i.e. trousers: 'Haud on till Ah put ma galluses on these winners an losers.'

Rhyming slang for first names

A certain amount of this exists but I have not included it in the foregoing list because it is not as widespread as the bulk of ordinary rhyming slang. It is recorded here for interest's sake.

Alabammy Sammy

Chanty Po Joe

Clydebank an Kilbooie Shooey, i.e. Hugh

Erskine Ferry, Finnieston Ferry, Govan Ferry Mary, in the local pronunciation as *Merry*

Esso Blue Hugh

Peas an Barley Charlie

Puff Candy Andy

Scapa Flow Joe

Sparkin Plug Shug, i.e. Hugh

Steak an Kidney Sidney

Scrappies' rhyming slang

Again, this is in limited use. My excuse for including it is that the few examples I have had drawn to my attention are both inventive and amusing. I am sure that similar specialist rhyming slang that I have yet to come across exists in other trades.

Dennistoun Palais Alley (short for aluminium)

Midnight Mass Brass

Missin Link Zinc

Pottit Heid Leid, i.e. lead

Phrases and Sayings

a blind man runnin for a bus wouldn't notice
Said jocularly of something that is considered good enough to pass a cursory inspection, having imperfections slight enough to make little real difference.

Ah could eat a farmer's arse through a hedge
Ah could eat a scabby dug
Ah could eat a scabby-heidit wean (between two bread vans)
All of these are meant to convey a level of hunger that compels one to abandon social taboos such as that against cannibalism as well as allow no difficulty to deter one in getting at the food.

Ah could sleep on the edge ae a razor
I am utterly exhausted, asleep on my feet.

Ah could sook the face right aff you
A fairly direct chat-up line, slightly more robust than 'give us a kiss'.

Ah don't know . . . the ticket's fell aff
A cheeky response on being asked belligerently what you are looking at by a person who believes you have been staring at him. The insult lies is comparing the person to an item in a shop window or a museum exhibit.

Ah never boil ma cabbages twice
I have no intention of repeating myself.

Ah'll see ye when ye're better dressed
A jocular farewell.

Ah'm meltin away tae a greasy spot
I'm far too hot or overworked.

Ah've lost merr runnin fur a bus
Used to contemptuously dismiss a paltry sum of money.

Ah've seen merr meat on a butcher's pencil
A male crack at a slim female; the kind of things shouted from a building site at women unfortunate enough to be passing by. Other variants of this are:
Ah've seen merr meat on a jockey's whip
Ah've seen merr meat on a well-chowed chicken bone.

Ah wish ye health tae wear it
A conventional remark addressed to someone who has recently obtained a new item of clothing.

Ah wouldny go oot wi um if hc fartit ten bob notes
He's not my type. Such a feat, which is not even impressive enough to win the speaker's affections, became still more unlikely with the introduction of decimal currency.

Ah wouldny pull it fur a pension
An obscene jibe from female to male.

all over the place like a cheap coat
Applied to anyone or anything that is seen in many different places.

am Ah right am Ah wrang?
A conversational interjection seeking the listener's agreement. The question is purely rhetorical as no-one actually expects to be told he is wrong: 'No way are that shower gauny win the league – am Ah right am Ah wrang?' 'Ye're right, son.'

another clean shirt an that'll be me (you, him, etc.)
A jocular statement made about the supposedly short life expectancy of a person who is mildly ill, perhaps complaining of a bad cough, and so on: 'How's that cold of yours?' 'Ach, another clean shirt an that'll be me.' Some people substitute simmit for shirt.

are you talkin tae me or chewin a brick?
A disrespectful response to being addressed by someone

you dislike or don't care to know. The punch is in the (often-omitted) next line: **either way ye're gauny lose teeth**.

a run round the table and a kick at the cat
If a harassed adult is preparing a meal and is continually pestered by children asking 'what's for my tea (or dinner, etc.)' he or she might reply with this phrase, which essentially means 'nothing at all'.

as deep and dirty as the Clyde
Said about a person considered unscrupulous, devious or secretive.

as high as a kite
Over-excited, unable to calm down: 'We couldny get the weans tae bed on Christmas Eve . . . they were as high as kites.'

as Irish as the pigs of Docherty
Unmistakably a product of the Emerald Isle: 'Imagine him thinkin ma mammy wis a Tally, an her as Irish as the pigs a Dochorty!' Just why Docherty's swine became a yardstick of Irishness I am at a loss to say.

as much use as a wet Woodbine
Of very little use whatsoever. Woodbine is, of course, a proprietary brand of cigarette.

as slow as a wee lassie
Applied to anyone considered dilatory.

as sure as guns (is iron)
Definitely: 'If ye don't get up this minute ye'll miss yer lift, as sure as guns.'

aw the nice!
An exclamation of pleasure at seeing something cute or sweet: 'Here's one of her in her first communion dress . . .' 'Aw the nice!'

better biled than fried
Said disparagingly of a scrawny person, usually by a male of a female: 'Ah'm no inty the skinny wan . . . she'd be better biled than fried.'

better grey hair than nae hair

A greying person's riposte to being teased about silver threads among the gold.

bite someone's ear

To approach someone for a favour, especially when trying to obtain something for nothing: 'See that jiner you know? Could ye bite his ear fur a bit a plywood?'

bother your shirt (or **arse, backside, bunnit** or **puff**)

What lazy or shiftless people do not do, i.e. make an effort, give a damn: 'Ye could've made a start while ye were waitin fur me, but ye didny bother yer shirt, did ye?'

breath like a burst lavvy

A withering description of the exhalations of a halitosis sufferer or of someone merely exhibiting one of the antisocial side-effects of a hangover.

by the way

This little phrase is notorious for turning up in every conceivable context, whether it belongs there or not. Like the similar tack-on expression **an at**, it has become a mere verbal space-filler or oral lubricant, helping actual relevant words to issue in a reasonably fluid manner: 'See that bag a messages, by the way? Gauny root through it an see if there's any a they thingmies an at in it.'

can't see green cheese

Said about anyone who seems to want a thing simply because someone else has it: 'She'll no be happy till she's got a T-shirt the same as his. That wean canny see green cheese.'

come in if your feet's clean

A jocularly irreverent invitation to enter someone's home, office, etc.

couldny hear him behind a caur ticket

A disparaging remark describing anyone who is either very small in stature or so quiet as to be insignificant. A caur, of course, is not a motor car but a tramcar, something not seen on Glasgow streets since the 1960s, and many people use an updated form of the expression: **couldny hear him behind a bus ticket**.

couldny run a menage

A menage (pronounced *menodge*) is a savings club in a place of work. To say that someone is incapable of being in charge of such a straightforward thing is to accuse him of utter incompetence: 'Ah don't know how that wee clown got to be a foreman. He couldny run a menage!'

There are a couple of other phrases with similar meaning: **couldny run a flag up a pole, couldny run a two-door shitehoose**.

couldny tackle a fish supper

Said of a footballer whose challenges are seen to lack bite, or more generally of anyone considered feeble.

could start a fight in an empty house *or* room

Said of someone who is naturally belligerent or loves argument for its own sake: 'It wisny ma Robert's fault. That boay a yours could start a fight in an empty hoose.'

daft as a ha'penny watch

Applied to anyone considered silly or eccentric.

did ye faw an break yer watch?

An ironic, ostensibly sympathetic, enquiry to a child who has fallen and, although obviously unhurt, is making a fuss.

doesn't know if it's New Year or New York

Said of anyone who is obviously not thinking clearly, whether because of being none too clever to begin with, or feeling the effects of an intoxicant or a shock of some kind: 'Ah wouldny bother phonin him at this time in the mornin. Even if ye get him up he willny know if it's New Year or New York.'

dogs always smell their own dirt first

Said to someone who complains of a bad smell, particularly if he is insinuating that a person in the company is responsible for it.

don't give us it

Don't expect me to believe that: 'Look, ye were seen winchin in the bus shelter, so don't give us it ye wereny oot last night.'

don't give us yer worries

Stop complaining or moaning: 'Ah wish ye would just dae whit ye're telt an no gie us yer worries.'

Similar requests include **don't give us the beef, don't give us the bully**.

do you think my head buttons up the back?

Do you take me for an idiot? The image is of a dummy or scarecrow, anything with a head that is empty and stuffed with padding.

frighten the French

Something that a striking or fearsome woman (and it does always seem to be a woman) is said to be able to do: 'Allow her! She'd frighten the French, that yin.' The assumption that the French are particularly brave is, I suppose, a product of the Auld Alliance.

get stuck in like two men and a wee fella

To eat heartily; often an invitation to do just that.

gie's peace

Stop bothering or irritating me: 'Will you two gie's peace wi aw that argy-bargyin?' It is possible to **gie yersel piece**, and a person who is thought to be worrying too much may be told to do so.

go off like a two-bob rocket

To lose one's temper very easily and spectacularly: 'All Ah says wis "How's yer love life?" an he goes aff lik a two-bob rocket!' The image is of a cheap (two-shilling) firework that, once lit, shoots fiercely if unpredictably up into the sky before fizzling out.

hair like straw hangin oot a midden

Said of any coiffure that looks untidy or unwashed: 'She goes aboot in the best a gear an her hair's like straw hangin oot a midden.'

A similar phrase is **hair like a burst couch**, comparing the crowning glory to the stuffing sticking out through a hole in a settee.

has emdy got a stick tae hit us wi?

An ironic rhetorical question posed by someone who is being verbally chastised and wishes to make the point that enough is enough.

have you been singin?

A jocular question asked of someone who is carrying such a lot of small change that he is suspected of busking in the street or in back courts: 'Wid ye look at aw the smash he's giein us! Have ye been singin, or have ye done the meter?'

he gets his shoes made at John Brown's

His feet are so large he has to have his shoes constructed at a shipyard

he had a bottom lip like the step on a corporation bus

He looked very disappointed or sulky.

hell mend you (**him, her** etc.)

Said to or about a person whose behaviour is likely to land him in trouble but who will not heed any warnings. I suppose the literal meaning is that if the person will not learn sense here and now he will repent at his leisure at the Bad Fire: 'Ye haveny listened tae a word Ah've said, have ye? Well, hell mend ye!'

he would drink it through a shitey cloot

A phrase applied to anyone so desperate for strong drink that circumstances that would deter the merely thirsty appear to present no obstacle to him. Other similar expressions include: **he would drink it oot an auld shoe; he would sook it aff a sore leg.**

hing aboot like a bad smell

To loiter around idly in a manner irritating to others: 'Gauny

go oot fur a walk or somethin instead a hingin aboot the hoose
lik a bad smell?'

hing aboot like a wet washin
To behave in a depressed or listless manner. This graphically
captures the image of a person physically drooping like wet
clothes on a washing line.

honey from the dunny
As a dunny is a basement or cellar in a tenement building, this
expression is a label stigmatising any woman who has come
from a rough background and who, although she may try to
maintain a veneer of sophistication, constantly gives herself
away: 'The manageress stays in Newton Mearns but Ah know
a honey fae the dunny when Ah see wan.'

hunger or a burst
Describes any state of affairs that is characterised by sudden
swings from a period of relative idleness or scarcity to a spell
of manic busyness or oversupply: 'Ah wish Ah wis in a steady
job. It's a pure hunger or a burst bein self-employed.'

if Ah don't see ye aboot Ah'll see ye a sanny
A parting witticism, playing on *aboot* as *a boot*, a *sanny* being
a sandshoe. There is also a suggestion of *see* to mean pass
or give.

if Ah don't see ye through the week Ah'll see ye through the windy
Another parting witticism; actually quite funny the first time
you hear it.

if at first you don't succeed, in wi the boot an then the heid
In this cheery message to anyone encountering difficulties,
the traditional 'try, try again' has been replaced by something
altogether more to local taste (and it rhymes as well).

if he was chocolate he would eat himself
A disapproving assessment of someone who has a high opinion of his own worth.

if it's for ye it'll no go by ye

A fatalistic catchphrase meaning what will be will be, that the events of life are somehow predetestined and cannot be avoided by personal initiative. It tends to be used when something unfortunate occurs or is anticipated.

it aw goes the wan way

Said with regard to different types of food being consumed, indecorously, at the same time: 'Ah pulled him up aboot stickin a Mars Bar on a roll an aw he says wis "It aw goes the wan way".'

it's nae loss what a freen gets

A conventional remark made by anyone who has given something to a friend, modestly deflecting any praise offered for the act of generosity.

it's no the cough that carries ye off, but the coffin they carry ye off in

A jocular catchphrase uttered when someone has a bad cough, not really meaning anything beyond a play on words.

it would bring a tear to a glass eye

Literally meaning that something is so moving that no-one can resist weeping, this phrase is more often used ironically to dismiss a claim for sympathy. A variation on the theme, but with considerably less logic, is: **it would bring a lump to a wooden leg**.

it would put a beard on ye or it would put years on ye

Said of something that is tedious or long and drawn-out. Each is an eminently down-to-earth way of putting over the idea that time seems to elongate when you are bored and you are made to feel as if a much longer period has elapsed than the real time taken: 'Gauny turn it tae The Simpsons? That snooker wid put a beard on ye.'

just swung doon oot a cherry tree

A phrase dismissing someone as not worth listening to: 'Never mind what he says. That diddy just swung doon oot a cherry tree.'

kiltie kiltie cauld bum

An irreverent jibe chanted by children at any male in High-land dress.

let the bull see the coo

Said by someone who feels he has the necessary expertise for a given situation and wants any bystanders to move out of his way: 'Oot ma road youse. Let the bull see the coo, till Ah get this sortit.' A similar phrase is **let the dug see the hare**.

like a fart in a trance

Applied to any distracted or listless person: 'Whit's the use a hingin aboot the hoose lik a fart in a trance? Away oot!' The relevance of *trance* is plain enough, but the concept of hypnotising anally-emitted gas is rather a surreal one.

like Sauchiehall Street

The name of one of the city's busiest thoroughfares is often applied to any bustling or crowded place: 'Ah'll come back an see ye when it's quiet. It's like Sauchiehall Street in here just now.' Some people substitute the equally busy Argyle Street.

like two plums in a wet paper bag

An appreciative description used by a male as he views an attractive female posterior. A similar expression, perhaps not quite so praiseful, is **like two puppies fightin under a blanket**.

looks like he drapt a bad E

Literally, he looks as if he has swallowed an impure Ecstasy tablet. This is used of anyone who looks nauseous or in a dwam: 'Is that the new manager over there? What's his problem? He looks like he drapt a bad E.'

looks like he's ready for a clap wi a spade

A rather callous remark made about someone who has the appearance of not being long for this world, having one foot in the grave, and so on.

mad as a wasp

Used to describe anyone who seems overexcited or a little

crazy: 'Gauny calm doon, you? Ye're mad as a wasp, so ye are!'

Madras in evening, mad arse in morning
A smart little play on words, usually delivered as a 'wise old saying', intended as a salutory warning against eating a curry that is hotter than you can handle.

must have been a lie
The standard retort to anyone who says he has forgotten what he was going to say.

my name is Gough and I am off
A remark made by someone who is about to depart, its poetry almost qualifying it as rhyming slang.

never died a winter yet
A farewell remark at the end of a conversation about life's difficulties, meaning that the person concerned has up to now alaways come through whatever tribulations have arisen.

no for havin it
Not in favour of something; not willing to put up with it: 'Ah fancy tryin Bulgaria this summer but she's no for havin it.'

nose runnin like a burn
A graphic description of one of the symptoms of a streaming head cold: 'That's me oot a hankies an ma nose is runnin lik a burn!'

not a pick on
Used in describing a person as over-thin: 'How in the name a the wee man does she need tae loss weight? There no a pick on her!' *Pick* in this sense (rather cannibalistically) means a morsel of food.

not enough to put in the corner of your eye
A very small amount indeed: 'Look at the wee bit a birthday cake they gannets have left for me . . . no enough tae pit in the coarner a yer eye!'

out with the sawdust
Used to describe anyone who is the last to leave a social event,
especially the last one out of the pub at closing time.

price of fish
Taken as a marker for inflation, this is frequently added to
complaints for emphasis: 'What wi this sore back an the price
a fish . . . ma life's no worth livin!'

refuse nothing but blows
To accept anything and everything that is going, short of a
gratuitous assault: 'Well, if ye're no wantin it, gie it tae me.
Ye know Ah refuse nothin but blows.'

say more than one's prayers
What an untrustworthy, and probably untruthful, person is
said to do: 'So that's whit she says, is it? She says more than
her prayers, that yin.'

smell of clay
When someone looks ill and may be considered as unlikely to
live much longer, a rather ghoulish observer might make a
remark along these lines: 'Did ye clock aul Morrison at the
purvey? Wi the smell a clay aff him it wis a waste a time him
gaun hame.'

so dae Ah, sodie watter
A contemptuous remark made to a person whose sole contribution to a conversation consist of merely saying 'so dae Ah
(so do I)' to any other individual's statements.

sufferin duck!
An exclamation, not meaning anything in particular, of exas-
peration, surprise, disbelief, etc. Variations on this include
sufferin Americans and **sufferin turkeys**. Why any of the
above-mentioned should be perceived as suffering more than
the rest of creation I cannot tell.

take the bad look off
To give a necessary improvement to the appearance of something: 'Ye'd think they'd give their front door a wee lick a

paint tae take the bad look aff it.' 'When Ah went in evrubdy wis up dancin except they two, sittin at a table full a drinks, an wee Boaby says "C'moan sit doon here an take the bad look aff us".'

that'll do me till Ah get somethin tae eat

A jocular remark made by someone who has just eaten a great deal and makes a joke of not being satisfied.

that really rips ma knittin

I find that exasperating in the extreme. Sometimes used for comic effect by speakers much too macho to ever have purled a stitch.

the band played 'Believe it if ye like'

A remark expressing doubt about the truth of another statement.

the man that et the belly oot the lodger's shirt

An unidentified individual, often blamed for any misdeed to which no-one will confess.

the nights are fair drawin in

One of those conventional conversational remarks used more often as space-fillers than for their literal meaning, which in this case is that it is starting to get dark earlier these days.

the one the cobbler killed his wife with

A humorous label for the last of anything, e.g. the last drink of the night, the last teabag in the packet, etc. The application is obvious when you consider what a cobbler is likely to use to murder his spouse: his *last.*

there's ma hand up tae God

An oath made to convince someone that you are telling the truth, often accompanied by physically holding up your right palm and placing the left, if free, over your heart. Also found in a shorter form: 'Ah'm tellin ye, hand tae God, no a word ae a lie.'

they're flyin low tonight

A code phrase, presumably dating from the war, used by one man to warn another that the zip of his fly is down.

thinks he's big but a wee coat fits him

A disparaging assessment of anyone who has an inflated opinion of himself, an example of a pronounced strain in Glasgow speech and attitudes: that of making sure everyone is cut down to size.

thinks he's honey an the bees don't know

Like the above, a remark made to pass comment on another's self-esteem.

to a band playing

Indicates a great willingness to take part in a particular activity: 'That wean a mines would eat grapefruit tae a band playin.'

toffs are careless

An observation made when someone is seen to be very generous or is spending a lot of money: 'D'ye hear what they rushed um fur that leather jaikit? Aye, it's well seen toffs are careless.'

The phrase is often used ironically when only insignificant sums are involved: 'Never mind the penny change, son. Toffs are careless, ye know.'

up Suckie, doon Buckie an alang Argyle

A walking route through the city centre that has become a catchphrase: up Sauchiehall Street, down Buchanan Street and along Argyle Street. When asked where they are going people often say this when they mean nowhere in particular.

up to high doh

Said of anyone who is overwrought or overexcited: 'The weans're always up to high doh on the last day of term.'

walk up and down till you're fed up

A remark intended to discourage someone from continually complaining about being hungry.

wan singer, wan song

Popularised by Billy Connolly, this catchphrase is supposedly shouted in a pub or club, etc when someone is trying to sing and others insist on joining in, to inharmonious effect. In everyday language it can also be heard as a call for order when a confused debate is going on: 'Hey yous, wan singer wan song, eh? Let the boay speak his piece.'

what's the crack?

A conventional remark equivalent to 'what's happening?' or 'what's going on?' Also used to request information on a particular topic: 'What's the crack wi these camera phones?'

whit d'ye want me tae dae . . . burst oot in fairy lights?

Said by someone refusing to be as impressed or excited as a person making some kind of announcement thinks he should be.

whit is it wi you?

A question, essentially meaning 'what makes you like this?', addressed to a person whose behaviour is annoying: 'Is this you moanin again? Whit is it wi you the day?'

who stole yer scone?

An unsympathetic question often addressed to someone who looks unhappy or aggrieved.

why are we so good?

A chant sometimes heard at football matches when supporters are so happy about their team's performance that they find it hard to comprehend why they are so blessed.

wouldny be held nor tied

A descriptive phrase used about anyone who is extremely agitated, angry or impatient: 'Ah wis late wi the wee soul's twelve o'clock feed. By the time she got her bottle she wouldny be held nor tied.'

wouldny be me

A stock assessment of a situation showing the speaker's disinclination to act similarly: 'Whit, marry a guy that's got weans already? It wouldny be me, pal.'

wouldny gie ye

These words appear as the overture to quite a range of phrases stigmatising meanness. Here are a few examples:

he wouldny gie ye a fright on a dark night
he wouldny gie ye a spear if he wis a Zulu
he wouldny gie ye daylight in a dark corner
he wouldny gie ye the itch
he wouldny gie a blind sparra a worm

wouldny make a back for a waistcoat

Said of someone considered very small or puny: 'The size a him, tryin tae jine the polis! He wouldny make a back for a waistcoat!'

wouldny say eechie or ochie

Wouldn't say one thing or the other; wouldn't say yes or no.

would ye credit it?

Would you believe it? This is so much of a catchphrase that it has been used, punning on the word *credit*, by companies advertising their easy-payment facilities.

yer jaws are gaun the right way

Literally, you are physically able to eat, this is used ironically by someone seeing another person eat heartily: 'Have another doughnut, wee yin. Ah'm that glad tae see yer jaws're gaun the right way.'

yer pie's in the oven

A phrase equivalent to **your tea's oot**, meaning you are in trouble now.

ye wouldny need tae be . . .

These words are used to begin phrases that mean 'it's a good thing that you are not . . .' For example: 'Ye wouldny need tae be easy offended when ye hear the language ae um.' 'Ye wouldny need tae be in a hurry, the time ye've tae wait oan this bus.'

Some of Yer Auld Patter

Many readers of *The Patter* and *The Patter – Another Blast* (as well as the previous edition of this volume) have written to me suggesting items of vocabulary that I chose not to include because they were not only too old-fashioned but often referred to things or places that no longer existed. While it remains my aim to document *current* Glasgow language, I feel it would be a shame to let some of these words and phrases be lost without record. For this reason I offer below a selection, by no means a comprehensive list, of older Glaswegianisms, many of which, as may be seen, spring from recollections of childhood.

as two-faced as the Briggait clock Very hypocritical.

Barlinnie drumstick A home-made weapon: essentially a pipe with nails in it.

Barney Dillon Rhyming slang for *shillin*, i.e. a shilling.

big picture The main feature in a cinema programme, in the days when a ticket bought you a supporting feature and a newsreel as well: 'What time's the big picture on?'

bundy A time-clock, as formerly used on tramcars to record journey times, etc.

caur A tramcar, often found in the plural **the caurs**: 'She got a job as a clippie on the caurs.'

clabber dance An informal dance held in a tenement back court (where participants would have to dance on *clabber*, i.e. dirt or mud). Apparently, people would hang carpets and sheets over washing lines to screen out wind and give the illusion of being indoors.

dollar Five shillings. **Half a dollar** was two shillings and sixpence, or half-a-crown.

doolander A wide flat bunnit, or man's cap, broad enough for a pigeon to land on.

figure To be **in one's figure** is to be lightly dressed, with bare arms, etc, as on a warm day: 'Ah see ye're in yer figure today, Mr Liston.'

Hairy-Leggit Irishmen A nickname for the HLI (Highland Light Infantry), many of whose recruits were Glaswegians.

half a toosh Half a crown.

Hi Hi, the A nickname for Third Lanark F.C., a well-supported former Glasgow team, based at Cathkin Park. Also known as **the Thirds**.

hunch-cuddy-hunch A street game played by boys, which involved climbing onto one another's backs.

KDRF A mischievous children's game, explained by the full form of its initial letters: Kick Door Run Fast.

kick the can A children's game, involving elements of hide-and-seek, in which the seeker must also prevent his prey from sneaking out to kick an agreed object, usually a tin can.

moshie A game played with marbles.

parish Someone who was **on the parish** was receiving unemployment or other benefits. To **join the parish** was to register for such benefits. These expressions date from a time when each individual parish was responsible for looking after its own poor.

pottit-heid bank, the The nickname by which a one-time bank branch in Govan was known because the pinkish hue of its sandstone stonework was reminiscent of the colour of the Scottish delicacy potted head.

ring-bell-skoosh Similar to **KDRF**, a game involving ringing a doorbell and running away.

Rottenrow, the The popular name for the Glasgow Royal Maternity Hospital, in Rottenrow. This famous institution, where countless Glaswegians first glimpsed the light of day, was closed in 2000.

Silent Death A ghoulish nickname for the electric trolley buses that plied the city streets between 1954 and 1967. Powered by overhead cables, these vehicles were so relatively noiseless that they could take unawares any citizen indulging insouciantly in the favourite Glaswegian pastime of jaywalking.

stankie A children's game of marbles that made use of the grille of a round stank as a playing surface, handy because the marbles sat neatly in the holes.

tartan banner Rhyming slang for a tanner, i.e. a sixpence.

thrummer A threepenny bit.

Tobermory tottie A sweetie, consisting of a chewy disc, dusted in cinnamon powder, inside which would be concealed a small plastic toy. A confection hazardous to the teeth in more ways than one. Also known as a **lucky tottie**.

winkle A penny (pre-decimal).